KNOW YOUR CHRISTIANS

Ten Missionary Pioneers

D1799407

By the same author:

Pilgrim's Programme

The Plain Man Looks at Himself

Him We Declare (with Bishop Bardsley)

Onward Christian Soldier (biography of S. Baring Gould)

Fisher of Lambeth (biography of Archbishop Fisher)

Woodbine Willie (biography of G.A. Studdert Kennedy)

Odd Man Out (biography of Lord Soper)

British Police in a Changing Society

A Time to Die

No Other Gods

Pilgrim's England

The Christian in Retirement

Martyrs of Our Time

Seekers and Finders (with Kate Purcell)

Evidence for the Holy Spirit

Comfort and Hope

Also in Know Your Christians series

– Ten Witnesses for God
– Ten Spiritual Leaders
– Ten Social Reformers

KNOW YOUR CHRISTIANS

Ten Missionary Pioneers

by
WILLIAM PURCELL
Canon Emeritus of Worcester

MOWBRAY
LONDON & OXFORD

Copyright © William Purcell 1987

First published 1987
by A.R. Mowbray & Co. Ltd,
Saint Thomas House, Becket Street,
Oxford, OX1 1SJ.

Typeset by Comersgate Art Studios Ltd, 52 St Clements Street,
Oxford OX4 1AG.
Printed in Great Britain by Cox and Wyman Ltd., Reading.

British Library Cataloguing in Publication Data

Purcell, William
Ten missionary pioneers.—(Know your Christians).
1. Missionaries—Biography
I. Title   II. Series
266'.0092'2   BV3700

ISBN 0-264-67129-5

CONTENTS

INTRODUCTION

A missionary is someone who is sent, and, more importantly for the purposes of the amazing stories in this book, who feels himself, or herself, to be sent by God to a distant land to do a particular job. That task, as the pioneers whose experiences are here recorded saw it, was to preach and teach and live the gospel of Jesus Christ so that as many as possible may be drawn to him. Now that our world has become something of a global village, where travel is easier and people know more of each other, and where something, maybe, of old certainties have faded away, this early idea of the missionary task may seem dated. In fact, the modern work of mission continues world-wide, though often it takes rather different forms from that which the pioneers followed. Maybe it is more sophisticated, maybe it accepts more of the value of other cultures. But one thing is certain; the christian story can produce no more heroic record than that of these pioneer men and women who, quite undaunted, faced incredible dangers and hardships in order to bear witness to the truth of the gospel.

SAINT FRANCIS XAVIER

(1506–1552)

Apostle to the East

It is difficult not to perceive Francis Xavier through a haze of sentimentality. He lived long ago, he is a saint, and many legends of an idealized life have been accredited to him. For instance, an image of him as reputedly seen by one of his companions describes him thus: 'He is a true father; no-one can see him without great consolation, the very sight of him seems to move to devotion; he is a man of middle height, he always holds his face up, his eyes are full of tears, but his look is bright and joyous, his words few and exciting to devotion. His very look kindles in men an inexpressible desire to serve God.' The real greatness of Xavier's work is obscured by this stereotyped picture of a saint. It is more challenging to strip the saint of his legend and glimpse the man beneath.

Born a Spanish aristocrat, Francis Xavier was the youngest son of Juan de Jasso, a noble of Navarre. He took the name Xavier from his mother who had brought her husband the properties of Xavier and Azpilqueta. From an early age he distinguished himself in his studies and, aged seventeen, was sent to the University of Paris where he was made a Master of Arts in 1530, and then lectured in logic and metaphysics. It was here that he met Ignatius

1

Loyola, who attended some of his lectures and became a great friend.

Loyola had, by that time, already decided on his vocation. A professional soldier, he was defending a breach in the castle wall of Pamplona against French invaders when a cannon-ball shattered his right leg. Left with a permanently mishapen limb, Loyola knew he would never fight again and gradually, during the long months of illness, felt drawn to consecrate himself to Christ. As soon as he was able he went on a pilgrimage to Jerusalem, stopping on the way to hang up his sword and dagger, symbolically, at the shrine of the Virgin at Montserrat: a knight dedicating himself to becoming a soldier of Christ.

On his journey Loyola formulated the rule of obedience which was to become the centre of his spiritual life. He wrote *The Spiritual Exercises*, a book in which he laid down a series of devotional meditations and instructions, whose aim was to train the will of the reader and to enable him to fully consecrate himself to the religious life.

After his pilgrimage to Jerusalem Loyola began to look for disciples who would join him in this supreme act of will. At first he was rejected and even imprisoned by the orthodox church, but in Paris he was able to find the first six men willing to join him in a brotherhood; one of the six was Xavier.

Loyola and his six disciples vowed to practise celibacy and poverty, to be both totally obedient to teaching and ordinances of the Church and totally obedient to the Pope as, in effect, its commander-in-chief. As well as this they vowed to devote the rest of their lives to apostolic labours. In a small chapel at Montmartre on 15 August 1534 the group formed the 'Society of Jesus' – the 'Jesuits' as they came to be called. Their first aim was to go to Palestine to work for the conversion of the Turks or, if this proved impossible, to offer themselves to the Pope to be sent on any work which he chose, however dangerous the mission might be.

It soon became clear that a mission to Palestine was impossible because war between Venice and the Turks blocked their passage. Although Xavier was interested in journeying as a missionary to the East Indies, the group decided to offer themselves to the pope. They began work in one of the northern Italian parishes, educating the children, preaching, working as chaplains to hospitals and conducting retreats. A papal bull of 1540 declared the object of the 'Society of Jesus' to be to propagate the faith, and this instruction was acted upon with such enthusiasm and success that the Society quickly grew in numbers, influence and range of activities, although it kept as its prime object its commitment to minister to the heathen and the poor, and to educate the children and illiterate.

Eventually Xavier was allowed his wish and on 7 April 1541, with three Jesuit companions, he embarked from Lisbon for the East Indies. He carried with him authority not only from the Pope but also from the King of Portugal. He was the pope's vicar for all the coasts of the Indian Ocean and he possessed the King's credence for his mission and an order from the King that all the Portuguese officials were to support him with all the means at their disposal.

The voyage lasted for sixteen months, including a

stay of six months at Mozambique. Xavier landed at last in Goa, India, on 6 May 1542. A nobleman of great charm and sophistication, he might have seemed an odd person to be sent as the first missionary to a foreign land far away from Portuguese court circles. However, his directness of character and simplicity, as well as his total commitment to missionary work, enabled him to enter fully into the strange life with great success. Xavier found Goa to be a great city with a cathedral and many churches and a monastery, such as might be found in any southern European town. But underneath the flamboyantly wealthy surface he found a chaotic muddle of differing cultures and beliefs. The Europeans had formed alliances with Indian women and the resulting children were left largely without care or education. The Europeans were also responsible for pressurizing the Hindu population to conform at least outwardly to Christianity, since 'idolatry' could not be tolerated in the territory of a christian sovereign. Not much progress had been made, however, in achieving much more than outward conformity. Xavier's first task was to attempt to reform Goa. He succeeded by revitalizing the churches, by establishing schools and above all by baptizing the children after teaching them the foundations of christian belief. Xavier believed that baptism was the most important part of his ministry: 'If you look round', he said, 'you will find that very few people in India, white or black, will reach heaven except those who die before they are fourteen years old, and so have not lost their baptismal innocence.'

A man of sudden decisions and enthusiasms, he was always eager to penetrate new ground, convert new tribes and face new danger. Soon he felt he must travel to South India to attempt the much larger task of baptizing the Parava fisher-folk of the Coromandel Coast. These poor, illiterate people had been suffering terribly from the depredations of Muslim raiders from the north and had, in desperation, turned to the Portuguese for protection. Protection was granted on condition that the population was baptized and in 1536, before the arrival of Xavier, the whole population of some ten thousand had been baptized en masse and then left for six years without instruction in the faith or pastoral care. This was to be Xavier's new area of work.

He found a rough, hardy people, good-natured, physically strong and dexterous in the handling of catamarans – their only source of livelihood. They lived scattered in small villages along the two hundred miles of coast, and as small metaphorically scattered christian islands isolated among the otherwise solidly Hindu population. They remained totally illiterate and without any knowledge of the christian faith into which they had been baptized. It was here that Xavier showed the real greatness of his character and work. Not having the miraculous gift of tongues with which he was later accredited, he relied on his interpreters to translate the Lord's Prayer, the Creed and the Ten Commandments. Then in each village he would gather the young people round him and teach them the christian elements by heart, after which he would set them to instruct the older members of the population. The Sunday service consisted of repeating the lessons as a kind of litany, as Xavier himself describes: 'On Sundays I assemble all the people, men and women, young and old, and get them to repeat the prayers in their language. They take much pleasure in doing so and come to the meetings gladly . . . I give out the First Commandment which they repeat, and then we all say together, "Jesus Christ, Son of God, grant us grace to love thee above all things." When we have asked for this grace, we recite the *Pater Noster* together and then cry with one accord, "Holy Mary, Mother of Jesus Christ, obtain for us grace from thy Son to enable us to keep the First Commandment." Next we say the *Ave Maria* and proceed in the same manner through each of the remaining nine Commandments. And just as we say twelve *Paters* and *Aves* in honour of the twelve articles of the Creed, so we say ten *Paters* and *Aves* in honour of the ten Commandments, asking God to give us grace to keep them well.'

Xavier found many difficulties among the Paravas, particularly their ignorance and unwillingness to change, and the corrupt lives of the Portuguese living on the coast. In spite of these obstacles he laid a firm foundation for the Church, and this achievement was entirely due to his open and sympathetic outlook towards other human beings, whatever their attitude or belief. He left the Paravas with churches, schools and, wherever possible, European priests: an extraordinary achievement for one man.

Xavier's commission from both King and Pope extended to the whole of the East and so he journeyed on to Malacca, the centre of Portuguese operations in the spice islands. Here he stayed for some months from 1546–47, but his eager mind was by now filled with plans for travelling to Japan. Perhaps he was attracted by the imaginative vision of that country as described by Marco Polo, who had never been there: 'Chipangu is an Island towards the east in the high seas, 1,500 miles distant from the continent; and a very great Island it is. The people are white, civilized and well-favoured. They are Idolators and are dependent on nobody. And I can tell you the quantity of gold they have is endless . . . Moreover all the pavement of the Palace, and the floors of its chambers, are entirely of gold, in plates like slabs of stone, a good two fingers thick; and the windows also are of gold, so that altogether the richness of this Palace is past all bounds and belief.'

Other reports of this strange country came from a group of Portuguese sailors who, in 1542, were driven off course by a storm and found themselves on the shores of an unknown land. Another source of information came from a man called Yajiro who had killed a man in Japan and to escape from justice had made his hazardous way to Goa. Here he met Xavier who wrote as follows: 'I asked him whether, if I went back with him to his country, the Japanese would become Christians and he said that they would not do so until they had first asked me many questions and seen how I answered and how much I knew. Above all, they would want to observe if I lived in conformity with what I said and believed. If I did these two things – answered the questions to their satisfaction and so demeaned myself that they could not find anything to blame in my conduct, then, after knowing me for six months, the King, the nobility, and all other people of discretion would become Christians, for the Japanese, he said, are entirely guided by the law of reason.'

Perhaps Xavier felt a sense of kindred feeling for these evidently superior people. At any rate he determined to travel to Japan, however difficult the journey, and to preach to the people there. It was with high hopes that he set sail from Malacca in a small junk belonging to a Chinese merchant. The voyage was a perilous one, as apart from the dangers of the sea, there was always the risk that, should the winds be unfavourable, Xavier and his companions might be thrown overboard as bringers of bad luck. In spite of all dangers, however, Xavier and his companions – two Jesuits, Yajiro and his Japanese attendants – arrived at the Japanese port of Kagoshima, Yajiro's native town on 15 August 1549.

Japan at that time was passing through a period of severe political disorder. There was no central authority but instead the land was divided up among two hundred and fifty Daimyos, or local rulers, each of whom claimed full authority for his dominion. No national bond of common religion united the divided country since Buddism was in discredit, so the country was open to new ideas as well as being eager for foreign trade. In these respects it was a propitious time to arrive in Japan.

Xavier, however, had placed too much reliance on his guide, Yajiro, who proved to be a broken reed. He had little knowledge of his own country, was not highly educated and was unable to translate christian terms into Japanese. Xavier realized, too late, that he had misplaced his trust in this Japanese man. Moreover, he and his companions had no idea of the severity of the Japanese winter and the cold which they had to endure. Worst of all, perhaps, was the daunting difficulty of the language: 'Now we are like so many statues amongst them', wrote Xavier, 'for they speak and talk to us about many things, whilst we, not understanding the language, hold our peace. And now we have to be as little children learning the language.'

In spite of all difficulties, friendship and understanding did develop and, in a letter of 5 November 1549, Xavier was able to write the following: 'Firstly the people whom we have met so far are the best who have yet been discovered, and it seems to me that we shall never find among heathens another race to equal the Japanese. They are a people of very good manners, good in general, and not malicious; they are men of honour to a marvel, and prize honour above all else in the world. They are a people of very good will, very sociable and very desirous of knowledge; they are very fond of hearing about the things of God, chiefly when they understand them . . . They like to hear things propounded according to reason; and granted that there are sins and vices among them, when one reasons with them, pointing out that what they do is evil, they are convinced by this reasoning.'

Most importantly and interestingly this contact with an ancient and noble civilization changed Xavier's concept of missionary work. Before, he and other missionaries had thought it necessary to level other beliefs which the natives might have in order to start afresh in building up a christian system of belief. This was the way Xavier had dealt with the simple fisher-folk, the Paravas. Now, confronted with a noble people, he saw that while the gospel could refine and transform, it was not necessary to reject as worthless everything that had come before.

Xavier stayed for twenty-seven months in Japan and left behind him three little groups of converts. A French scholar summed up what the missionary had achieved in that short time. 'With remarkable penetration he had grasped the social and political situation in Japan and had settled on the methods which could ensure success . . . He had understood that, if this proud, intelligent, logical people with its passion for disputation was ever to be won, it would be necessary to send missionaries of the highest quality, flexible enough to adapt themselves to the customs of the country to the limit of what was permitted by their faith, but strong enough in character to fashion their conduct according to the rigid requirements of the faith which they taught.'

At the end of 1552 Xavier began his return voyage to India, and soon after his return to Goa, set out to preach the gospel in China. This time, however, he did not receive the usual help from Portuguese officials, and after long delays he decided to set out on his own in July 1552. After stopping at Singapore, he reached the island of San Chan, one hundred and twenty miles from Canton in August. Here he had to wait again for a ship to take him on to Canton and, while he was waiting, became ill with a fever.

He died aged forty-six, reputedly murmuring the words of the *Te Deum*, 'In te Domine speravi, non confunder in aeternam': 'O Lord, in Thee have I trusted, I shall never be confounded.' But before the mists of sanctity obscure Xavier again, another image of the man may be superimposed; the image of a man with extraordinary gifts of charm and intelligence which enabled him to draw people to him, even those of different cultures and beliefs; and a man with gifts of curiosity and energy which drove him on to explore and preach in foreign lands far away.

WILLIAM CAREY

(1761–1834)

The Call of India

At the first public meeting of the Baptist Missionary Society a minister reported that 'On 5 October 1983 I baptized, in the River Nene, a little beyond Dr Doddridge's meeting house in Northampton, a poor journeyman shoemaker, little thinking that before nine years had elapsed he would prove the first instrument of forming a society for sending missionaries from England to preach the Gospel to the heathen . . . and that . . . later he would become the professor of languages in an Oriental College and a translator of the Scriptures into even different tongues.' He was referring to William Carey, a co-founder of the Baptist Missionary Society who, until his decision to break away from being a nominal member of the Church of England and become a baptist, lived quietly in the village of Paulerspury near Northampton.

Born the son of the village schoolmaster, Carey left school at the age of twelve in order to earn his own living. He became apprenticed to a shoemaker in a nearby village and here met another, older apprentice who had recently been converted to the non-conformist baptists and was eager to share his faith with Carey. 'He became importunate with me, lending me books . . . which gradually wrought a change in my thinking and my inward uneasiness increased',

Carey related in later years.

After his baptism, Carey continued to read, teaching himself Latin and Greek and continuing his apprenticeship. At the age of eighteen his master died and Carey transferred to another shoemaker in the nearby village of Hackelton. Here, at the age of twenty, he married an uneducated girl, Dorothy Plackett, and here, in the same year, his new master died and Carey took on the business as well as providing for his old master's widow and four children. Needing to increase his income, he opened an evening school, at the same time increasing his knowledge by reading anything he could borrow or buy. He particularly enjoyed teaching himself languages and once borrowed a copy of *Captain Cook's Voyages* which offered him a glimpse of strange places, customs and people. His awakening desire to learn was constantly excited by the events of the time: the American Independence, the rumblings of impending revolution in France, the trial of Warren Hastings in India. Carey became fascinated by the far-away places of the earth. He made himself a leather globe in different colours, as well as a wall-map of the world, and began teaching himself French, Italian and Dutch.

Carey continued to teach at his school and began preaching with such success that he was soon invited to become minister at the local baptist church. But the content of his preaching was not always acceptable to local baptist church-goers. Carey had come to believe passionately through his study of foreign countries, that Christ had a kingdom which should be proclaimed to the ends of the earth. The majority of his congregation believed conversely that the conversion of the heathen would be the Lord's own work in his own time and that nothing could be done by men to hasten it. Carey, zealously studying languages for which he had a natural aptitude, and relinquishing his job as shoemaker and teacher to give himself time to enlarge his knowledge, was not to be dissuaded.

At last, in 1792, Carey was ready to publish a pamphlet which incorporated all his ideas. Entitled *An Enquiry into the Obligation of Christians to use Means for the Conversion of the Heathen*, it was a patient, methodical survey of the world and of the whole history of christian efforts to bring the gospel to it. The appeal of this pamphlet was reinforced by Carey's sermon to a group of baptist ministers at Nottingham on 31 May 1792. Starting from the text of Isaiah 54: verses 2–3, 'Lengthen thy cords, and strengthen thy stakes', he proclaimed his two great principles: 'Attempt great things for God; expect great things from God'. As a result of this powerful declaration, a famous resolution was passed by the baptists which read: 'Resolved that a plan be prepared against the next ministers' meeting at Kettering for forming a Baptist Society for the propagating of the Gospel among the heathen'. Carey had won: he had persuaded the baptists of the need to spread the gospel, and four months after that famous sermon the Baptist Missionary Society was formed. In June 1793 Carey left for India, having decided, after deliberation, that the Indian continent was 'a gold mine' waiting to be converted. He left with his family, as the Society's first missionary, reaching the Hoogly River on 11 November of that year. The day of the English-speaking peoples in overseas missions had begun.

Carey's arrival in India was not greeted with

enthusiasm by the East India Company, which was in the process of transforming itself into the dominant power in India; its uncertain control of the country made the Company suspicious of any other foreign influences, such as missionaries. Carey and his party were able, however, to disembark without opposition, and made their way to Calcutta where they sold the goods that had been brought as a trading venture. Carey had with him John Thomas, a baptist convert who had been to India before and could speak Bengali, and he and Carey begun to visit the natives, Thomas preaching and Carey listening and learning the language.

But money ran out; Carey's family became ill, and his wife began to show the first signs of what was to become permanent mental illness. The house in which they were living in Calcutta was a dilapidated ruin in a marshy, malarial area of the town. Besides this, the appalling poverty of the people of Calcutta almost overwhelmed Carey; he realized that without funds and without help he would be unable to make any improvements. At this low point in Carey's career he was offered a post as manager of an indigo plantation by a friend of John Thomas. The salary was generous, a house was provided and Carey would have time to become fluent in, and to translate the Bible into, Bengali. The plantation was a twenty-three day journey by river from Calcutta in the interior of the country, and Carey and his family were relatively safe from transportation by the East India Company – always a risk while they remained in Calcutta.

The family, however, continued to suffer, one of the boys dying of fever, Dorothy becoming increasingly ill mentally and Carey, himself, ill much of the time and feeling very lonely. He wrote in his journal: 'February 3, 1795. This is, indeed, The Valley of the Shadow of Death to me. . . O, what would I give for a sympathetic friend to whom I might open my heart. . .' To add to his depression, letters arrived from England criticising his decision to become a plantation manager; he and Thomas were cautioned 'not to engage too deeply in the affairs of this life lest it should dampen their ardour, if not divert them from their work'. This hurt Carey deeply and he replied, 'Whether the spirit of the missionary is swallowed up in the pursuits of the merchant it becomes me not to say. Our labours will speak for us . . . the love of money has not prompted me to this indigo business. I am poor indeed and always shall be till the Bible is published in Bengali and Hindustani, and the people need no further instruction.'

At the end of five years as manager of the plantation, Carey had completed his translation of the New Testament into Bengali, but there was another, even greater unhappiness. He found that, when tested, the translation proved to be unintelligible. Carey, a self-taught man with an untrained gift for languages, had mastered the Bengali vocabulary but not its idiomatic use.

Showing the indomitable persistence which had given him impetus all his life, Carey determined to begin again from the beginning. At this time of near despair, his situation was radically altered by the arrival in 1799 of a group of missionaries, sent out to reinforce Thomas and Carey from England. Among them were Joshua Marshman, a schoolmaster, and William Ward, a printer who, with Carey, were to

16

unite to form a famous missionary team. Marshman and Ward realized that their safety lay in settling at Serampore, a tiny Danish colony sixteen miles from Calcutta. The Danes did not share the hostility of the British to missionaries and they would be free from the constant uncertainty of life on British soil. They persuaded Carey to join them and from then on his life in India took root and blossomed.

'Serampore', wrote Carey, 'is a handsome place; populous, well-ordered . . . healthful'. It was here that the team bought a large house in the middle of town and soon established a routine, described by William Ward thus: 'About six o'clock we rise; brother Carey to his garden; brother Marshman to his school at seven; Felix', (Carey's eldest son), 'and I to the printing office. At eight, the bell rings for family worship. We assemble in the hall, sing, read and pray. Breakfast. Afterwards, brother Carey goes to the translation, or reading proof; brother Marshman to school and the rest to the printing office. . . We print three half-sheets of 2000 each a week. . . At twelve o'clock we take a luncheon; then most of us shave and bathe, read and sleep before dinner which we have at three. After dinner we deliver our thoughts on a text or question; this we find to be very profitable. Brother and sister Marshman keep their schools till after two. In the afternoon, if business be done in the office, I read and try to talk Bengali with the Brahmin. We drink tea about seven, and have little or no supper.

'We have Bengali preaching once or twice in the week and on Thursday we have an experience meeting. On Saturday evening we meet to compare differences and transact business after prayers, which is always immediately after tea.'

The team saw their aims as missionaries as a five-pronged advance; the wide-spread preaching of the gospel by every possible method; the support of preaching by the distribution of the Bible in the language of the country; the establishment of a church; a clear understanding of Indian fellow-workers. All these aims were achieved with some success, but the production of Carey's bible is undoubtedly the most notable.

On 5 March 1801 the first bound Bengali New Testament was completed, the product of seven and a half years' work and scholarship, and this time the translation proved worthy of Carey's hard work. Its printing and distribution marked the beginning of a gigantic enterprise; in thirty years six translations of the whole Bible were completed and Carey was responsible for Bengali, Sanskrit and Marathi. In addition, twenty-three complete New Testaments and parts of the Bible in ten other languages were produced. Carey continued to revise his translation as well as providing grammars and dictionaries; a self-taught scholar whose diligence and enthusiasm for linguistics led to his position as the leading authority on languages in the Far East.

But besides the fame which Carey won for these achievements, other missionary initiatives undertaken by the team proved equally successful. Preaching tours were carried out in all directions, stemming from Serampore and radiating far afield up the Ganges, to Orissa, and even as far as Burma where Carey's eldest son, Felix, became the pioneer missionary. A church was established at the Serampore mission settlement and William Ward elected pastor. The church, although baptist, of course, and therefore distantly connected with the baptist church in England, was independent and formed an integral whole with the mission. Because of this, converts to Christianity at Serampore were in no way tied to a 'mother church' in a far-away land.

This sensitivity to the independence of the natives extended to the understanding which Carey and his team developed for, not only the language, but the thought-processes of the Indians. Realizing that the missionary must fully understand the country of which he is a part, Carey not only translated the Bible for the Indians but also an Indian work, *The Ramayana*, for the English. Ward also contributed a book on the manners and customs of the Hindus.

The final aim of the team, that 'of forming our native brethren to usefulness', was achieved eventually by the opening at Serampore in 1819 of a 'College for the instruction of Asiatic, Christian and other youth, in Eastern Literature and European Science'. The college opened with thirty-seven students, nineteen of whom are christian and eighteen non-christian. In 1827 the King of Denmark gave the college a charter with the power to grant the degrees of Bachelor of Arts and Bachelor of Divinity.

Carey was assisted in the success of all these ventures by his appointment as a tutor in languages at Fort William College in 1801. This recognition of his stature both as a linguist and as a missionary brought him into contact with influential Englishmen of Calcutta and, in spite of fluctuations in the East India Company's opinion of missionaries, Carey was able to use his influence to promote numerous social reforms. He initiated research into the Indian practice of widow-burning, or *sati*, and found to his horror that it was common custom to burn wives alive on their husband's funeral pyre. He determined to abolish this practice, but for a long time no authority, not even Lord Wellesley, Governor of India, could outlaw the cruel custom. After years of patient campaigning, Carey was finally called upon by the new Governor-General, Lord Bentick, to translate an edict into Bengali, declaring the rite illegal and criminal.

Perhaps a less major achievement, but nevertheless a step forward for humanity, was Carey's fight against the cruel treatment of lepers, who were regarded as social outcasts and left to die. He initiated the building of a hospital for lepers in Calcutta, and so established a precedent for the sympathetic care of leprosy. He also became passionately interested in botany, and published the *Botanist's Flora Indica* which became and remained a standard botanical work. Carey's eclectic mind encompassed still other areas of Indian life and, as early as 1811, he wrote a paper on the cultivation of timber and followed this with more extensive research into agriculture, founding in 1820 the Agricultural Society of India. He expressed his sadness that '. . .in one of the finest countries of the world the state of agriculture and horticulture is so abject and degraded and the peoples' food so poor and their comforts so meagre.' The Agricultural Society slowly began experiments in the growing of coffee, cotton, tobacco, sugar-cane and some cereals, as well as inventing methods of irrigation and fertilization.

Carey's devotion to India was total. Surviving

until the age of seventy-two, he outlived all of the original members of the missionary team, as well as two successive wives. He never returned to England but died on 9 June 1834, having asked to be buried next to his second wife, Charlotte. He requested in his will that nothing was to be inscribed on his tomb but his name, the dates of his birth and death and two lines of an old hymn:

> A guilty, poor and helpless worm
> On thy kind arms I fall.

DAVID LIVINGSTONE

(1813–1873)

The Call of Africa

The body of Livingstone lay in state for fourteen days, guarded ceaselessly by African natives who wailed their requiem:

> Today the English man is dead,
> Who has different hair from ours:
> Come round to see the Englishman.

He had died on his last pilgrimage in search of the source of the Nile, in a roughly thatched hut on the edge of the Bangweolo swamps at Ilala, in what is now Northern Zambia. After Livingstone's death, his heart and viscera were buried in a tin box under a tree while his native friends embalmed his body, wrapped it in the bark of a tree, lashed it to a pole and hoisted in onto the shoulders of bearers for the nine-month long march to the coast. At last the body of the poor boy from Glasgow was transported back from Africa to a hero's funeral in Westminster Abbey.

David Livingstone was born in Blantyre, Lanarkshire, and brought up in a single room fourteen feet by ten in a three-storey tenement. Here he lived with his four brothers and sisters and his parents, Neil and Agnes. Neil was an itinerant tea-vendor; 'too conscientious ever to become rich', as David wrote of him later. The family were intensely religious, Neil being deacon at an independent congregational church at Hamilton three miles away. At the age of ten David went to work as a cotton-piecer and with his first week's wages bought a Latin textbook, propped it against the frame of a spinning-jenny and learnt from it as he worked. 'I kept up a pretty constant study undisturbed by the roar of the machinery', he wrote. His desire for learning was enormous. He was able to continue his studies with a schoolmaster after working in the factory from 6 a.m.–8 p.m.; at home he was always reading or roaming the countryside with *Culpepper's Herbal* as his handbook, thus laying the foundations of a knowledge of natural history that was to remain a lifelong interest.

As a young man of twenty, Livingstone felt a deep need to enter actively into the service of God: 'In the glow of love which Christianity inspires, I soon resolved to devote my life to the alleviation of human misery.' He decided to qualify as a doctor and go as a medical missionary to China. Continuing work at the factory in the summer, he began to study medicine at Anderson's College in Glasgow, then moved to London to enrol as a probationer with the London Missionary Society. His clumsy preaching won him adverse reports; 'his heaviness of manner, united as it is with rusticity, not likely to be removed', commented the Principal, adding that 'his temper is good and his character substantial . . . I trust he will prove . . . an instrument worth having.' Livingstone, having qualified as a missionary, continued his medical studies in order to become a doctor, working both at Moorfields and Charing Cross Hospitals. While lodging in London he met one of the great missionaries of Africa, Robert Moffat, who persuaded him to relinquish ideas of working in China, partly because opium wars were making it difficult to enter China, and to sail with him instead for Africa on 8 December 1840.

David Livingstone was then twenty-eight years old, a qualified doctor as well as a christian minister, his deepest ambition 'To preach beyond another man's lines'. Eager to discover 'the smoke of a thousand villages' beyond Moffat's headquarters at Kuruman, in what is now called Botswana, Livingstone immediately embarked on a long journey – one thousand miles into the interior – with several objects in mind: to study the language of the natives by cutting himself off from European society, to gain a knowledge of their diseases and to select a site for a new mission station. Early in 1843 he camped at a village where the chief of the local Bakwena tribe lived. His only son was ill with dysentry and Livingstone was able to cure him and also to become a friend of the chief, Sechele. It was Sechele who fired Livingstone's imagination by pointing north towards the Kalahari Desert and saying: 'You never can cross that country to the tribes beyond, it is utterly impossible even for us black men, except in certain seasons when more than the usual supply of rain falls.' The idea of attempting to cross this desert and to visit the reputedly powerful and benevolent chief, Sebituane, never left Livingstone, although two events occurred which might have changed his mind. Firstly, while on a hunting expedition, he was badly mauled by a lion and had to return to Kuruman to be nursed, and secondly he married the nurse – who happened to be Robert Moffat's eldest daughter, Mary.

Married in 1845, David and Mary Livingstone travelled extensively together, living in rough mud huts, often encountering hostility from the natives as they attempted to survey the mission-field. Mary made their bread, soap, candles and clothing; Livingstone discovered slowly that most natives had 'not the smallest love for the gospel of Jesus'.

By 1849 the Livingstones were tired and dispirited, but David retained his determination to cross the Kalahari and meet Sebituane and, in the company of his good friend William Oswell, who financed the expedition, he set off and managed to cross the desert in spite of nearly dying of thirst. Sebituane reputedly lived two hundred miles north of Lake Ngami which Livingstone and Oswell succeeded in reaching on 1 August 1849. The lake, lying on a route to the unexplored interior 'beyond another man's lines' excited Livingstone intensely, but the lakeside natives were unfriendly and refused to supply guides or food, so the expedition had to turn back.

On his second attempt to reach Sebituane Livingstone took his family, though Mary was pregnant and they had, by this time, three children under five years of age. They started on their journey, accompanied by Sechele but not by Oswell, in April 1850. However, it was sickness caused by lakeside mosquitoes which proved the reason for turning back this time; two of the children and nearly all the expedition members being ill with fever. The whole family set off again in 1851 and again with Oswell, this time leaving Lake Ngami on their left and plodding northwards, their water-bottles almost dry and their oxen exhausted. The children were suffering; '. . . the less there was of water, the more thirsty the little rogues became. The idea of their perishing before our eyes was terrible'. Just in time they reached the swampy watershed where Sebituane's territory lay. The old chief came to greet them and at first seemed ill at ease. Later, in the middle of the night, he visited their camp-fire and, according to Oswell, 'He dreamily recounted the history of his life, his wars, escapes, successes and conquests and the far-distant wandering in his raids. By the fire's glow and flicker among the reeds, with that tall, dark, earnest speaker and his keenly attentive listeners, it has always appeared to me one of the most weird scenes I ever saw.' A fortnight later he died suddenly in total ignorance of the existence of Christ. 'Alas! alas! Sebituane. I might have said more to him. God forgive me,' mourned Livingstone.

While waiting at camp for permission to proceed on their journey from Sebituane's heir, Livingstone came to a momentous decision; he would penetrate the unknown interior down to the west coast – a distance of about eighteen hundred miles. The family must be sent back to England where they would be properly looked after. Livingstone did not make this decision lightly, 'Nothing but a strong conviction that the step will tend to the Glory of God would make me orphanize my children', but he believed that 'it is the will of our Lord that I should, I will go, no matter who opposes.'

He left Kuruman in December 1852 with three ox-drivers, a single wagon and a minimum of provisions. Returning to Sebituane's territory he found that the tribe under their new leader, Sekelutu, had planted a garden for him in the hope of his return. He and his men pressed on into the unknown, travelling by canoe at first, then hacking their way with axes through thick, dripping undergrowth. Livingstone was frequently ill with malaria until he was reduced almost to a skeleton and, too weak to walk, had to ride astride an ox. At last the team reached the Portuguese-held territory of Angola: it was 31 May 1854 when Livingstone's native bearers first saw the sea: 'We marched along with our leader believing that what the ancients had always told us was true, that the world has no end; but all at once the world said to us, "I am finished, there is no more of me." '

Livingstone decided to accompany his natives back to Sekelutu instead of returning to England. The return journey was extremely difficult as he was ill for a great deal of the time with a severe attack of rheumatic fever, but he was given a hero's welcome by Sekelutu and learnt the news that he had been awarded a Gold Medal from the Geographical Society for his mission of exploration.

Livingstone and the chief, Sekelutu, then left on 3 November 1855 for the east coast. This expedition was easier, there was better food and the climate was not so harsh. Livingstone, however, felt the threatening presence of the slave-trade as local tribesmen, fearful of being captured, gathered near the camp, clearly intending to attack. To divert the tribesmen's attention, Livingstone showed them his watch and other novelties while the rest of his men embarked hurriedly in canoes. This episode caused Livingstone much grief, as did the sight of the ruins of an old church with its cross and broken bell. 'O Jesus', he prayed, 'See . . . how the heathen rise up against me as they did to thy Son.' Eventually, Livingstone reached Quilemane where, instead of feeling that his mission to open up both east and west Africa had been accomplished he recorded, 'I view the end of the geographical feat as the beginning of the missionary enterprise'. The next step, he thought, was to establish inland, permanent settlements of Europeans who would build up the country's wealth by building up honest trade, as well as end the slave-trade.

Returning to England in 1856 after an absence of sixteen years, he found himself a national hero. Africa had become fashionable: the Dark Continent had been opened up by Livingstone and other explorers and had revealed something for everyone – scientists, geographers, businessmen, philanthropists, all had an interest in the vast continent which was both a challenge and a mystery. Besides speaking publicly about his explorations, Livingstone was able to enjoy a reunion with his family. This did not last long, however.

The steam ship, *Pearl*, left Liverpool on 12 March 1858. On board were Livingstone, his wife, and the members of his expeditionary team, all financed by Parliament. The aim of the expedition was to explore the source of the Zambesi river, to conduct agricultural experiments and to give religious instruction to the natives. In fact, the mission was to last six years instead of two and was to bring disaster to the party as well as triumph.

The first disappointment to Livingstone was that Mary was again pregnant and so had to be left with her parents at Kuruman instead of accompanying him on the expedition. The second was that the Zambesi river was too shallow to accommodate the *Pearl*; a paddle-steamer had to be used instead. This was far from satisfactory, being small, uncomfortable and consuming great quantities of wood. On reaching the Kebrabasa rapids, Livingstone was dismayed to find that they seemed completely unnavigable – perhaps it would not be possible to explore the source of the Zambesi after all. He ordered from England a more powerful ship capable of navigating the rapids. Meanwhile morale was low; everyone suffered constantly from fever and quarrelled amongst themselves. Livingstone continued to make sorties from the base at Tete, discovering the fertile and beautiful Shiré highlands rich in mineral resources, and setting eyes on Lake Nyasa – the expedition's major geographical find. He established a small mission in Shiré: it was, as he saw it, an ideal place for a settlement. But as if to counteract this success came the realization that Livingstone's actions in opening up the interior were spreading the slave-trade. On this expedition gangs of native captives would frequently be found, their necks fastened with forked sticks, burnt villages and rotten corpses left as silent witnesses to past raids. But at last the expedition members intervened, and, frightening away the slave-traders, cut the slaves free. From that time on they freed all the slaves they came upon. Retaliation by the raiders was inevitable; they often had to be driven off with musket fire.

More powerful ships had by now arrived, one of them bringing Mary. However, disaster struck: the people at the mission in the Shiré highlands died suddenly of fever and Mary shortly after this contracted the disease herself and died. She was buried under a baobab tree in April 1862, aged forty-one years.

After this, Livingstone's desire to progress up the Zambesi became an obsession. Time after time he would make attempts, always failing because of the impossibility of the task and the unfriendliness of the natives. At last the ships managed to navigate up to the Shiré valley, once so richly cultivated. Now sickness and the slave-trade had devastated the area: 'Dead bodies floated past us daily, and in the mornings the paddles had to be cleared of corpses caught by the floats during the night', wrote one of Livingstone's team.

The expedition, having lasted three times as long as planned, was recalled. Livingstone, after some delay, arrived at Mozambique, determined to sell one of the expedition's ships, the *Lady Nyasa*. However, he would not sell to the Portuguese who might use her to transport slaves, so instead he decided to sail her across the Indian Ocean to Bombay, taking with him as crew nine natives who had never been to sea and three naval ratings. Amazingly, after forty-four days at sea they anchored at Bombay: 'We had sailed over 2,500 miles. The vessel was so small that no-one noticed our arrival,' recorded Livingstone. He did not sell the ship after all: selling it, perhaps, seemed like selling his stake in Africa. Instead he paid his crew and embarked for England which he reached on 23 July 1864.

After a year in England, he left for what was to be his final journey, in August 1865. His mission, this time, was to discover the secrets of the unknown, unmapped country around Lake Nyasa, although Livingstone still claimed he saw himself as a missionary who 'did geography by the way'. However, at the back of his mind was the belief that, with

God's guidance he would this time discover the origins of the three great African rivers, the Zambesi, the Congo and, above all, the Nile.

Familiar difficulties recurred: lack of food, illness, the presence of slave-raiders and the quarrelling of members of the party. At Lake Nyasa some mutinied and left the party having stolen many provisions and one of their number returned to Zanzibar and convinced the consul there that Livingstone was dead. Flags were flown at half mast and obituaries filled the newspapers. A year later though, Livingstone's letters giving an account of the mutiny proved this statement to be untrue. Livingstone, meanwhile, zig-zagged west, then north, crossing deep ravines and hacking his way with his party through forests of bamboo: 'The country is a succession of enormous waves all covered with jungle and no traces of paths', he wrote. Eventually they reached the immense watershed of the Congo river system and the southern tip of Lake Tanganyika. Livingstone was seriously ill with rheumatic fever by this time and had lost his medicine chest, but instead of making for the town of Ujiji where he had ordered medicines and supplies to be sent, he decided to work his way up the western side of the lake to find out whether it narrowed. On he and his team laboured, squelching and wading through mud and water, often ill and often lost, Livingstone still believing that he would soon discover the source of the Nile. But ferocious tribal wars blocked his way and he was carried, with acute pneumonia, to Ujiji, only to find that no supplies had arrived.

Astonishingly Livingstone's health recovered and he again set out to find the source of the Nile, this time travelling west of Tanganyika. Ill and lonely, 'in agony for news of home', as he wrote, he struggled on but again tribal fighting forced him to retreat to Ujiji. Now, having run out of all supplies, he was destitute and almost friendless.

One morning on 10 November 1871 a luxurious caravan was seen approaching, bearing the American flag. It was Henry Morton Stanley, and the famous greeting, 'Dr Livingstone, I presume', fell on thankful ears. Stanley and Livingstone had much to tell each other and became good friends. They set off on an expedition together to explore the northern end of Lake Tanganyika and continue Livingstone's quest for the Nile source, but lack of supplies and men made it necessary for Stanley to leave Livingstone and trek to the coast to replenish and send supplies back. After their sad parting, Livingstone never set eyes on a white man again.

After five months of waiting, men and supplies arrived, sent by Stanley. Livingstone's last expedition set off, encountering unprecedented wet weather which continued month by month as the team waded through the leech-infested marshes. Livingstone was again ill, this time bleeding from the intestines; 'Rain, rain, rain, as if it never tired on this watershed . . . I must plod on', he wrote. Too weak to walk, he was carried on the shoulders of his men: the nightmare continued for eight months, canoes capsizing, the team exhausted. At last Livingstone wrote, 'I am excessively weak'. Carried in great pain to a hut, he was laid gently on a bed of sticks and grass. On 1 May 1873 he was found kneeling by his bed. His final journey had ended.

MARY SLESSOR
(1848–1915)

Woman among the Wild Tribes

Shortly before David Livingstone's death he wrote a letter home which was published by the Scottish newspapers. The letter read: 'I direct your attention to Africa. I know that in a few years I shall be cut off in that country which is now open . . . Do not let it be shut again. Do you carry out the work I have begun. I leave it with you.' To the twenty-five year old Mary Slessor, Livingstone was a hero. Born and raised in the slums of Dundee, Mary had from an early age been inspired by a sermon given by a missionary, home from Calabar, about the fearful conditions created by the slave-trade in Africa. From then on she began to borrow copies of *The Missionary Record*, read about David Livingstone, and realized his similarity with herself. Like her he had been a mill-worker, like him she would read books while she worked at her loom. Soon she had educated herself enough to be able to teach in the local Sunday School.

The local minister, James Logie, gave Mary encouragement at this time. Noticing her strong personality, her gift for communicating, and above all her tough invincibility, he recommended that she apply to the Foreign Missions Board for a place as 'female agent' in Calabar. This was an unusual idea since women missionaries, or 'female agents' as they were called in Scotland, were usually educated ladies from the professional classes. However, Mary applied, was accepted, trained, and on 5 August 1876 she said goodbye to her family and set out from Liverpool on the SS *Ethiopia*.

A month later Mary saw the mission at Duke Town, Calabar, for the first time: the old sailing ships in which the white traders lived moored in the anchorage, the red clay walls and yellow thatch of the clustered mud huts which made up the town. She was taken to the white mission house high on a hill overlooking Old Calabar below. The mission had a staff of thirteen, some Scottish and some Jamaican. The reason why the mission always included Jamaicans on its staff was that the Scottish Mission Society working in Jamaica had decided to repatriate some of the slaves from their country so that they might teach Christianity to their fellow countrymen. Their original intention had been to set up a completely African church, but the Efik tribes of Calabar were firmly pro-British and wanted to learn 'white man's fashion' in order to compete on better terms with European traders. As one of them, 'King' Eyamba put it: 'Now we settle for not to sell slaves I must tell you some thing I want your Queen to do for me . . . some man must come for to teach book proper and make all men saby God like white men . . . also I want bomb and shell.'

The slave-trade along the coast of Calabar had brutalized the tribes; the chiefs had grown used to looking on human beings simply as merchandise and when in 1833 MacGregor Laird, a famous explorer, visited Calabar, he described it thus: 'The most uncivilized part of Africa ever I was in . . . I was much struck by the demoralization and barbarism of the inhabitants . . . The human skulls seen in every direction and that are actually kicking about the streets attest the depravity of feeling among the people.' By the time Mary Slessor arrived in 1876, however, the original missionaries had persuaded the chiefs to put an end to human sacrifice and ritual killings in and around the Calabar towns, but penetration into the interior, away from the trading stations and protection of the Efiks, was known to be impossible: 'If you do [attempt this] your lives will not be worth a moment's purchase', warned a trader.

But it was the interior which fascinated Mary and drew her to itself; the beauty of the jungle and the narrow winding paths which led through immense trees to the primitive villages of the Efik tribe excited her. By contrast, life at the mission station became more and more difficult. One reason for this was that she found herself unable to fit into its conscious life of etiquette; the Sunday afternoon tea-parties which it gave for white traders, the, as she termed it, 'proper' behaviour of the other missionaries. Mary's life was made far more miserable, however, by her detestation of Efik customs. She particularly loathed the way in which woman and children were treated: they had no rights and the male head of the household was able to do what he liked with his own family, even kill them. In the eyes of Efik males the fatter the woman the more beautiful she was, so at puberty she was cooped in a fattening-house where she was fed special foods and allowed no exercise. If after her marriage her husband should die, her fate would be either to accompany him to the spirit world or to be put into a widow's mourning-shed where she was starved and prevented from washing so she became covered with sores and vermin. Perhaps the most brutal Efik custom was their killing of twins. Believing that one twin was always the child of a devil which secretly mated the mother, the Efiks felt it necessary to kill both the babies while the mother was driven out of the tribe. Mary was so upset by this particular custom and so determined to rescue the twins from death that she would make lonely journeys through the bush, sometimes at night, to rescue them. Soon she had a roomful of orphans to nurse and feed and although she suggested that the mission establish a central orphanage, it failed to carry out her idea and she was left to care for them on her own.

Mary felt increasingly drawn to the unknown quantity of the interior, particularly to the Okoyong tribe who, as another missionary wrote, 'rejoice in a wild freedom and this feeling, with their distrust of each other, separates them so that each family has its own settlement in the bush, living a life of thorough independence . . . All the customs of blood which have been abandoned in Calabar still prevail amongst them.'

Just why Mary, who detested the savage customs of the Efiks, should want to live among a tribe far more savage, is hard to understand. Probably the part-Westernization of the Efiks repelled her and she felt she would be of more use living amongst a tribe which had never known a missionary: moreover, she always felt drawn to the poor Africans rather than those concerned with cultivating Western manners for their own material benefit. Most importantly, she had a special gift of entering instantly into a life different from her own: 'The people found her different from other missionaries, she would enter their townships as one of themselves, show in a moment that she was mistress of their thought and ways, and get right into their confidence,' reported the editor of *The Missionary Record*.

Eventually Mary was given charge of the Calabar mission at Old Town. Now on her own she was free to try out her own ideas about mission-work. Leaving the orphans in charge of African girls whom she had trained, she was able to spend days and nights in the villages sleeping on a clay bench in a hut as the local people did. She began to make night journeys along the narrow paths through the bush, something few people except head-hunters or raiding parties would attempt. Hearing the snarls of hunting leopards, she persuaded the Efiks who carried her medicine chest to sing, and prayed: 'Oh Lord of Daniel shut their mouths'. The chief of the Efiks (who had become very fond of Mary) lent her his canoe and one day, although warned by natives of Old Town of the dangers she was about to face, Mary set out to visit Okon, chief of a tribe thirty miles distant. It was dusk by the time the party set out and reed torches were lit which glittered in the water as the paddles dipped to the rhythmic beat of a drum and the crew chanted: 'Our beautiful Ma is with us, Ho! . . . Ho! . . . Ho! . . .'

Although the Okon tribe had never seen a white woman before they soon treated her with respect, even obeying her when she appealed against the flogging of two girl-wives of one of the chiefs. The sentence – a hundred lashes with a rawhide whip for being caught in the hut of another man, was reduced to ten lashes each. Mary's friendship with the Okon was such that the chief escorted her back to Old Town in his own canoe and the success of the venture made Mary even more determined to visit the Okoyong tribe which had always fascinated her.

Inevitably, after these years in the Calabar, Mary became ill and had to be sent home to recuperate. She took with her a little girl, one of a pair of twins whom she had saved and who was to become in later years Mary's friend and helper, 'My wonderful Jean'. At home she found both her mother and her two sisters suffering from tuberculosis and became their nurse for a time, reluctantly leaving home, after a few years absence, to return to Africa. Back at Old Town, a year after her return, the news came that her mother and sisters had died. Now Mary had no 'home'. She wrote to a friend, 'I, who all my life have been caring and planning and living for them, am left . . . stranded and alone . . . Heaven is now nearer to me than Britain and there will be no-one anxious about me if I go up country.'

She determined, not only to visit the Okoyong but to live with them and although her colleagues were aware that she was taking an appalling risk and would almost certainly be killed, they gave their permission for her to go. The Okoyong agreed without much enthusiasm that she might come to live amongst them, perhaps because, being a woman, they saw her as having no power and therefore unlikely to influence them in any way.

On 4 August 1888 Mary moved to the Okoyong village of Ekenge, accompanied by most of her orphans. At first conditions were wretched; she was given an old leaking hut in which to live, the floor was muddy, rain poured down on her boxes of luggage and bedding. More important than her physical surroundings was the need to establish herself with the tribe, always remembering that if they disliked her they would probably murder her and claim she had been killed by head-hunters or leopards. Mary began by treating the sick and injured among the women and children and one day was sent an important patient, one of the wives of the chief. 'He had bitten her during the orgies at a funeral feast, and the native witch doctors having done their best, he begged me to take the case in hand' she reported. The septic wound soon responded to Mary's treatment and the chief and his wife were most impressed, as were the rest of the chiefs. As Mary said, 'From this my fame spread far and wide . . . with all their faults they are not insensible to kindness . . . After this I had many visitors from the interior towns . . . everyone laid aside his arms at the entrance to our yard and everyone gave us an invitation to spend a week or two at his place.'

Unpredictably, Mary's popularity did not last long. One of the chief's concubines had fallen in love with a slave and gone to his hut to persuade him to run away with her. Knowing the terrible penalties, he refused and had gone to work: the girl went into the forest and hanged herself. But she had been seen entering his hut and he was accused of enticing her with *Ifot* (witchcraft). He was sentenced to be flogged and executed but Mary, protesting that the sentence was unjust, confronted the tribe on his behalf. The angry tribe, amazed at her interference, shouted and waved guns and swords at her. 'Things got critical', Mary wrote later. Seeing, however, that she continued to stand her ground in the midst of them they realized that they were making no impression on her and calmed down. The chiefs condescended to argue the case with Mary and compromised by reducing the sentence to flogging only. Mary had now become not only a medical worker but an advisor. But her position with the Okoyong was still very uncertain. To teach her that their judgements were not to be interfered with lightly, the chiefs chained the slave to a post in the yard behind her hut and flogged him for three days. Through the mud wall Mary could hear his screams and moans but could not go to him because sentries prevented her.

For a long time after this Mary worked towards her acceptance within the tribe. She began to teach 'Book' – the Bible – and also taught the eager students to read and write Efik, the language most useful for communicating with other tribes, and European arithmetic, which would be useful for trading. When the natives realized the progress they were making, their suspicion of Mary gradually faded away.

Mary's deep understanding of the African mind enabled her to fit into the life of the tribe. She and they were alike in several ways; her belief in God was the same as the Okoyong belief in an omnipotent presence which they called *Abassi*; the poverty of her childhood had prepared her for the life she now led; her sense of humour matched theirs. At last, when the chief of the tribe built her a house of her own, Mary knew that she belonged to the Okoyong. Before long she became known by the Okoyong and surrounding tribes as *Eka Kpukpro*

Owo – 'Mother of All the Peoples'.

Mary lived as one of the Okoyong tribe for many years, suffering their hardships with them – their tribal warfare, their witchcraft – ill with fever much of the time. Since no other missionary would replace her, believing the work to be too dangerous, she 'drudged on', as she termed it. Her fame spread and one day in 1893 she had a Western visitor, Mary Kingsley, the woman explorer who had arrived in Calabar 'in search of fetishes and fish', as she said. Determined to visit 'Miss Slessor' she made her way by canoe to Ekenge, a revolver in her handbag and a dagger concealed on her person in case things got too uncomfortable. As she arrived, Mary Slessor was in the process of rescuing twin babies who had been born in a nearby village and the uproar was such that the guide suggested she turn back: 'I think not', said Miss Kingsley, 'Miss Slessor is expecting me'. She summed up her time at Ekenge thus; 'Some of the pleasantest days of my life . . . this very wonderful lady . . . her abilities both physical and intellectual have given her among the savage tribe a unique position and won her, among many white and black, a profound esteem.'

Soon afterwards a terrible epidemic of smallpox swept through the Calabar region. Edem, chief of the Okoyong, was one of the victims and Mary, returning after some time from vaccinating babies in more remote areas, found a pile of dead bodies in her yard while the dying waited for *Ma Akamba*, as they called her, to cure them. This time even she could not work a miracle: going to Edem's hut she found him dead and deserted; the best she could do for her old friend and protector was to bury him under the floor of his hut with, as was customary, his sword, gun, chief's staff and whip.

For the rest of her long life Mary travelled further and further into more remote areas. She repeatedly wrote to the Mission Society asking for help but only a few missionaries came to join her and her adopted daughter, Jean. It seemed, as W.P. Livingstone said, as if Mary alone was 'dragging a great Church behind her' into Africa. At last, after thirty-nine years in the Calabar, *Eka Kpukpro Owo* died of a fever, heart disease and malnutrition, aged sixty-seven years. Attended by her beloved Jean she murmured to the God of the Okoyong, 'O Abassi, sani mi yok' – 'O God release me', and died. Wailing women and a steady drumbeat summoned the tribes of the Efik, Okoyong, Itu and many others, who escorted her body by canoe down river to Old Calabar, where the flags flew at half mast. The whole area grieved.

ALBERT SCHWEITZER

(1875–1965)

Reverence for Life

Response to life: reverence for life. These are two key phrases which provide an initial insight into Albert Schweitzer's formidable personality. He described his philosophy of life thus: 'With consciousness and with volition I devote myself to being. I become an imaginative force like that which works mysteriously in nature, and thus I give my existence a meaning from within outwards.'

To attempt to understand the man and his life it is necessary to re-tell the famous story which he always used when illustrating how he arrived at his big decisions and convictions. Aged nine years, he was walking with a friend one spring morning in the fields near his home town of Colmar, Alsace: 'We got close to a tree which was still without any leaves and on which the birds were singing beautifully, to greet the morning . . . stooping, like a Red Indian hunter, my companion put a bullet in his catapult and took aim. In obedience to his nod of command I did the same, though with terrible twinges of conscience. . . At that very moment the church bells began to ring, mingling their music with the songs of the birds and the sunshine . . . for me it was the voice of heaven. I shooed the birds away . . . the music drove deep into my heart: Thou shalt not kill. From that day onwards I took courage to emancipate myself from the fear of men, and whenever my inner convictions were at stake I let other peoples' opinion weigh less with me than they had done previously.'

This says much about Schweitzer the man; his process of sudden passionate discovery, a period of thought followed by undeviating action. As he grew older this same process led his independent mind first to question and then to follow Jesus, who became to him a tragic hero, a figure who had taught an ethic of brotherly love and had voluntarily taken it upon himself to endure the tribulations of mankind in the hope of seeing the coming of a new order. As a student Schweitzer saturated himself in Jesus, a man searching for the mind and motives of a man. His love and emulation of Jesus was never to deviate. It is true to say that, in fact, he gave his life for Jesus, feeling as he believed Jesus to feel that 'we should all take a share of the burden of pain that lies upon the world.' There is a specific moment when Schweitzer's recognition of the raw material of Jesus in humanity dawned upon him. As a student he attended a course of lectures on the history of missions. He wrote later: 'I was struck for the first time by the idea of expiation. It has an extraordinary effect on me . . . launched as an appeal to work under the banner of Jesus, this word took on life, it was a cry, a shock, something which sank into you and took hold of you and as that day ended I understood Christianity better, and I knew why missionary work was needed.'

Experience once again was followed by decision, decision by action. 'Proceeding to think the matter out at once with calm deliberation, I settled with myself before I got up, that I would consider myself justified

44

in living till I was thirty for science and art, in order to devote myself from that time forward to the direct services of humanity.'

This momentous and never to be abandoned decision was taken when Schweitzer was twenty-one. He had nine years to decide what 'direct service' he would offer humanity. For the moment, his life was packed with passionate commitment to theology and music. Since a child, Schweitzer had shown great talent as an organist and, now a student of theology in Strasbourg, he had progressed to such an extent that he was already an authority on Bach. Taken on as a pupil by the internationally famous organist Charles-Marie Widor, Albert was able to combine organ-playing, which, as Widor said, 'is the manifestation of a will filled with a vision of eternity', with his search for an understanding of Jesus and his own personal religion.

The brilliant student, prompted by Theobald Ziegler to complete his degree by studying the philosophy of Kant, moved to Paris where the library was more comprehensive and where he would be able to see more of Widor. Here he became a protégé of the great organist and managed in three years to complete his thesis, which Ziegler pronounced to be a work of genius. Now he had to decide which avenue to take, theology or philosophy. Schweitzer, influenced perhaps by his father, decided on the first course. He would become ordained for 'preaching', he wrote, 'was a necessity of my being.'

And so it was that Schweitzer became a minister in Strasbourg, combining the life of a pastor with that of a philosopher and musician. Only a year after his ordination, the principal of Strasbourg's Theological College died. Schweitzer was chosen as his replacement. This was an extraordinary move for a newly-ordained man and coincided with the publication of his first book, *The Problem of the Last Supper*, together with *The Secret of the Messiah and his Passion; a Sketch of the Life of Jesus*. Schweitzer's ruthless logic and his refusal to compromise meant he upset many christians with his controversial arguments about the fallibility of Jesus. Some theologians protested against his retaining his post of Principal. However, Schweitzer continued to hold both his position and his beliefs. He defined himself as follows: 'There are two sorts of Christians – the dogmatic and the undogmatic. The latter follows Jesus and accepts none of the doctrines laid down by the early Church or any other Church. That's the sort of Christian I am.'

By the autumn of 1904 Schweitzer had been Principal of the college for three years and only had three months before his thirtieth birthday. He had to make a decision: what 'direct service' would he offer humanity? Quite by chance he opened a magazine lying on his desk and read the title of the article: 'The needs of the Congo Mission'. As he wrote, 'The conclusion ran: "Men and women who can rely simply on the Master's call, 'Lord, I am coming', those are the people whom the Church needs". The article finished, I quietly began my work. My search was over.'

One day in 1905 Schweitzer slipped an explosive fistful of letters into a Paris letterbox, announcing to his unsuspecting family and friends that, 'at the beginning of the winter term I shall enter myself as a medical student, in order to go later on to Equatorial Africa as a doctor.' Another letter resigned his post as Principal of the college. This was a traumatic time for Schweitzer; he had shocked and horrified everyone who knew him with his decision and he found it difficult to explain: 'My friends have no more patience with my paradoxes. It's time for me to go', he said. For the next six years he trained to become a doctor, feeling that preaching the religion of love was not enough; the people of Africa must see him practising it. To finance his studies he turned to organ-playing, giving concerts of Bach all over Europe and returning to Strasbourg on the night train. He toiled on, his greatest difficulty being to stay awake hour after hour during medical lectures. On 17 December 1911 he qualified as a doctor. Now only two parts of his plan remained incomplete; one to take a course in tropical medicine, and the other to marry his long-time friend, Hélène Bresslau.

On Good Friday, 13 March 1913, Albert and Hélène left their families and boarded the train for Bordeaux. It was hard to leave but it would, for Schweitzer at least, have been harder to stay: his whole life had been in preparation for this moment.

The long voyage from Bordeaux to Cape Lopez in the Gulf of Guinea was followed by a journey by river steamer and canoe up the Ogowe River to the mission station at Lambaréné. 'So it goes on hour by hour', wrote Schweitzer; 'Always the same forest and the same yellow water. . . It is impossible to say where the river ends and land begins, for a mighty network of roots, clothed with bright-flowered creepers, projects right into the water.'

It was here at Lambaréné, hemmed in by the immense forest under the beating sun, that Schweitzer set up his first clinic for natives decimated by the slave-trade and inter-tribal warfare. He had been taught what diseases he would encounter but he had never imagined that the sick would be so numerous. Every morning he would find, waiting for him on his verandah, thirty or forty negroes suffering from 'skin disease of various sorts, malaria, sleeping-sickness, leprosy, elephantiasis, heart complaints, dysentry, venereal disease. Truly, as one old chief said, "our country devours its own children." ' Besides physical diseases Schweitzer had to contend with psychological complications; taboos, curses and the dread of witch-doctors. It was urgent to construct a makeshift hospital and this he and Hélène did, using a dilapidated chicken hut. Hélène sterilized the instruments, assisted at makeshift operations and cared for the patients. Luckily, an unusual patient arrived who was to make up the third member of the medical team. This was Joseph Azowani, who had trained to be a cook and now offered to act as interpreter and medical assistant. Although he had his peculiarities referring to various sections of the patients' anatomy as if they had been pieces of meat, ('This woman has a pain in her upper left cutlet, and her loin'), he was reliable, intelligent and loyal and remained with the Schweitzers for a number of years.

By the autumn the Mission Society agreed to provide money for the building of a more permanent hospital. It was no more than a shed of corrugated iron on the bank of the river divided into two rooms, one of which Schweitzer used for examining patients, the other of which he used for operations. Another hut provided the sleeping places. At last some sort of order had been established, although Schweitzer had to live with constant anxiety, mainly because he could not remove himself physically or mentally from the suffering of the patients. 'I have not the robust temperament which is desirable in this calling', he admitted. 'Pain is a more terrible lord of mankind then even death himself.' His only retreat from stress was to play the piano brought laboriously up river for him to set himself the task of learning Bach's works by heart.

By the summer of 1914 the Schweitzers were exhausted and planned a trip home in the spring of 1915. It was not to be: Europe went to war and on 5 August they were informed that, as German citizens, they were regarded as prisoners of war. They were placed under house-arrest and Schweitzer was forbidden to practise as a doctor. Suddenly he had much time to think. Believing that the war was the result of western civilization's long decay, he sought for a basic human principle which would underwrite the validity of human ideals. As usual he found his answer suddenly, passionately, and after he had found it never deviated from it. 'There flashed upon my mind, unforeseen and unsought, the phrase "Reverence for life". The iron door had yielded, the path through the thicket became visible.' In a sense Schweitzer's life, ever since the incident with the catapult as a boy, had led towards the discovery of this phrase, but its articulation satisfied both his instinct and his intellect. He determined that, for the rest of his life, he would live and preach this ideal.

A year later the Schweitzers were allowed to practise medicine again, but in 1917 were suddenly told to pack and leave for an internment camp in France. They were sent first to a camp in the

Pyrenees, then to Saint Remy, until they were listed as prisoners to be exchanged and sent home to Germany; a Germany much changed: 'There were dull roars from guns on the mountainsides. . . Houses ruined by gunfire. Hills which I remembered covered with woods now stood bare. . .'

But the war ground to a halt at last and the Schweitzers established themselves in a house near Albert's old parish of Saint Nicholas. It was here that their first and only child, Rhena, was born in 1919. Yet Schweitzer knew that his work lay unfinished at Lambaréné and that somehow he must return there. He determined to give organ recitals and lectures in order to build up a fund for his work and in this he succeeded beyond his wildest hopes. Between 1920 and 1924 he played and lectured all over Europe and saved enough money to reopen the hospital in Lambaréné and to build a house for Hélène and Rhena in the Black Forest, since Hélène's health prevented her from returning to Africa.

On 21 February 1924 Schweitzer embarked on his second voyage to Lambaréné. It had been six and a half years since he last saw his mission hospital. Now, roofless and overgrown, it hardly existed: the jungle had reclaimed the building.

Work began to rebuild from the beginning, but a combination of catastrophes; a new type of dysentry which did not respond to the doctor's drugs, a prolonged rainy season – all made it clear that the site of the old hospital would never be adequate. Schweitzer and his by now expanding team must move two miles up river where the land was far more favourable. He was given one hundred and fifty acres of land at Adoninalongo, enough space to grow food for the patients as well as to house lepers in their own colony, to provide separate buildings for seriously and mentally ill patients and to house a laboratory. Now, with the building of the new hospital, the fame of Schweitzer's work grew, and doctors, nurses and builders began to arrive, eager to help. Finally, in 1927, a fleet of canoes moved the patients to the new hospital. 'For the first time my sick were housed as elementary humanity requires', he wrote.

Schweitzer returned home shortly after this, partly to see Hélène and Rhena, and partly to raise funds for the hospital. By the end of the lecture-tour he was established as a legendary figure, an embodiment of his own philosophy 'Reverence for Life'. He had set out to make his life his argument and was now presenting his argument to the world. As his fame grew so did the, at times, hysterical adulation of his audience, '. . . the terrific impact of his presence . . . a riot of people surging round him . . . a veritable tornado,' describes one of his biographers.

Schweitzer returned to Lambaréné, this time taking Hélène with him, although ill-health prevented her staying long. The expanding community was full of life and growth: it had become not solely a hospital, but had grown into a village; a community of all life. These pre-Second World War years were probably the most personally fulfilling of Schweitzer's life: he took upon himself the role of headman of the village, peasant on his farm, superintendent of his hospital and pastor to his flock. 'I restrict myself to the simplest experiences', he wrote. 'Whatever my point of departure, I always

51

come back to the central idea; letting oneself be seized by Christ.'

Shuttling between Lambaréné and his European tours, Schweitzer would return again and again to his beloved African community, laiden with honours, and more importantly, funds. Then came the Second World War: Europe was closed to Schweitzer but funds kept trickling in from America, Britain and the Swedish Red Cross. Although he had to limit the number of cases he admitted to hospital because of lack of staff, Schweitzer managed to keep going during the difficult war years. In 1945, as hostilities ceased, he wrote in his diary, 'Weapons are disastrous implements. . . The slaughter of human beings in great numbers should be lamented with tears of compassion.' But the slaughter was not over: evidence that man had discovered the opposite of 'Reverence for Life' was not long in coming as, on 6 August 1945, the first atomic bomb was dropped on Hiroshima.

In 1954, aged seventy-nine, Schweitzer received the Nobel Peace Prize. The theme of his acceptance speech reiterated his long-held belief that organizations can never, by themselves, bring about peace. What humanity needed, he said, was 'a new attitude of mind, an attitude based upon ethics'. Schweitzer was persuaded to write and broadcast against the proliferation of the arms race. He broadcast in 1957 his 'Declaration of Conscience' in which he urged the public to exercise its individual voice and reason with their respective governments to stop the testing and stock-piling of atomic weapons.

Schweitzer had, indeed, become the embodiment of his own philosophy and Lambaréné had come to epitomize his philosophical ideal. He died quite suddenly at Lambaréné, aged 90, on 4 September 1965. Always believing that life should be spent in the service of love in its widest sense – *caritas* – he passed on a message to all who wish, as he did, to express their feelings of humane and human impulses; 'You can have your Lambaréné anywhere'.

HUDSON TAYLOR

(1832–1905)

The Call of China

James and Amelia Taylor married in 1831 and began to pray together for a son whom God would use for the evangelization of China. In their chemist's shop at Barnsley they read Exodus 13:2 about the conversion of the first-born, and they dedicated their own to God. They named him James Hudson and lived, not only to see their prayers answered, but to bear witness to the growing success of the mission he founded.

James, or Hudson as he was always called, grew up in a zealously religious home. His father was a passionate lay preacher and took his son with him when he spoke at meetings; daily he knelt with his family, praying for them each by name and his characteristic expression, 'He cannot deny Himself, He would not be God if He could', was the belief by which Hudson came to live and the cornerstone of the China Inland Mission which he founded.

Hudson Taylor's interest in China stemmed both from imbibing the missionary spirit of his parents and their associates, and from reading, at the age of eleven, Peter Parley's book *Ching and the Chinese*. The author's excitement and enthusiasm leapt from the pages; 'one of the most interesting nations on the face of the earth. If I had called it the most wonderful, I should not be far from the truth . . . It is the oldest government . . . the most populous nation. . .'

From then on Hudson Taylor's obsession with China grew, fanned by a conviction that he was, as he said, 'the finished work of Christ', and the knowledge that 'we have the promise that ALL shall know Him whom to know is life eternal.' He began to teach himself Chinese and to read, avidly, issues of *The Gleaner in the Missionary Field*, which bolstered his determination to become a missionary and to save, as he saw them, the heathen Chinese in remote parts of China who were dying without God.

Hudson sailed to China as a member of the Chinese Evangelization Society in 1853. One of his first acts was to become as much like the Chinese as possible. To this end he wore Chinese clothes, grew his hair long and in a pigtail or *bianzi* as it was called, ate their diet and lived in a typical Chinese house. In this respect he differed markedly from many other missionaries in China who lived in western-style houses and lived western-style lives, employing the Chinese as servants. Mrs Mary Simcox, wife of the Reverend Frank Simcox of the American Presbyterian Mission, described her residence thus: 'we have got our new carpet down in the dining-room, our organ in the lounge, my writing-desk, sewing machine . . . also a small table with some pretty silver inkstands on it. . .' Whereas many missionaries were proud of their status as representatives of a major imperialist power, Hudson Taylor questioned this attitude: 'Why should such a foreign aspect be given to Christianity?' he asked. 'The Word of God does not require it, nor, I conceive, could sound reason justify it. It is not the denationalization but the Christianization of this people that we seek.'

From the beginning other missionaries regarded Hudson Taylor as an oddity, partly because of his adoption of native habits and partly because he was not an ordained minister or a doctor. He had no special qualifications, only a burning desire to convert the Chinese. This he attempted to do for four years, travelling from Shanghai to make a base at Ningbo and from there penetrating into the interior, preaching and living among the natives. He soon became dissatisfied with the Chinese Evangelization Society, because they failed to support him either morally or financially. In 1857 he wrote his letter of resignation: 'You feel you owe me a fixed sum every quarter, which your funds do not enable you to send and monies sent to me . . . I do not feel free to use. For these reasons I relinquish my salary entirely. If [the Lord] see fit to supply my need in some other way the glory be ascribed to Him alone.' For a time after this he lived without the underpinning of any missionary society, simply in trusting God. He continued work in Ningbo with a group of other independent missionaries and described a typical day thus in a letter home: 'Our public services, three times a day are generally attended by some who are interested . . . passers-by come in and go out . . . ask questions and offer objections . . . we trust to see fruit, and believe that the day of Christ will reveal many cases where the good seed has borne fruit to the glory of God.' But for a long time the seed did not bear fruit; the missionaries became ill, depressed and exhausted. Besides all this, Hudson Taylor had fallen in love with a young girl called Maria Dyer, but her aunt and guardian was opposed to the friendship between her niece and the eccentric young missionary who dressed like a native

56

and had no money or qualifications. However, the aunt eventually consented to their marriage and in 1858 they began life together in Ningbo.

The next few years were ones of hardship, poverty and illness. The average life-expectancy of a missionary was only seven years and, for the small colony at Ningbo, death struck again and again. Yet no one regretted their life: 'if we had to choose again, we would choose just this work in this place', one testified. Hudson's own health deteriorated – he had constant bouts of fever and dysentry while Maria had been very ill with typhoid fever. Financially they relied on Maria's small inheritance and literally trusted in the Lord for gifts of money from well-wishers to keep them alive. Hudson Taylor felt that his work lay in the hospital at Ningbo helping the doctor, but he did not realize that he would soon have to run the hospital single-handed; the doctor's wife died and the bereaved family left for England. Hudson remained in sole charge, keeping the hospital open and dealing with all kinds of illness. As he wrote, 'a number of persons shot or wounded by pirates were brought into the hospital . . . One of these, a boy of about eighteen, was shot through the neck,' recovered, and was then converted to Christianity. Hudson was also earning a reputation for breaking opium addiction and the development of this work had a sequel: a conscience-smitten opium dealer donated three thousand pounds to Hudson so that the China Mission Society might open a hospital for opium addicts.

Work grew and multiplied. Hudson wrote home urging his father to influence the Wesleyan Church to send out more missionaries; 'If I had a thousand pounds, China should have it. If I had a thousand lives, China should have them. NO! not CHINA but CHRIST.' He formulated a principle of recruitment on which he was to act when he returned to Britain; 'anyone qualified to labour amongst the poorest and most ignorant rustics of England needs only God's blessing to make him as useful, or more so, here . . . we do need many labourers of this class. Persons who, from the way they have been accustomed to live, are ABLE to endure labor and hardship.'

In 1860 Hudson Taylor, Maria and their children were forced, through ill-health, to return to England. Here, Hudson Taylor soon recuperated and was able in the following five years to qualify as a doctor, to recruit volunteers and to raise money. Hudson Taylor had reckoned that 'a million Chinese a month were dying without having known God', and that, to save as many Chinese souls as he possibly could, he needed 'twenty-four willing, skilful labourers'. In the event, he and Maria sailed for China with fifteen recruits of mixed social class and ample funds from the lecture tours Hudson had made; their aim being to open their own mission; 'The China Inland Mission'. They sailed in the *Lammermuir* on 26 May 1866, waved off by a crowd of enthusiastic well-wishers who had been drawn to Hudson Taylor's magnetic personality during his five years of lecturing on China. An Irish evangelist, Grattan Guinness, wrote a commemorative poem for the occasion:

Over the dark blue sea, over the trackless flood
A little band has gone in service of their God.
The lonely waste of waters they traverse to
    proclaim
In the distant land of Sinim Immanuel's
    Saving Name.
They have heard from the far-off East the
    voice of their brothers' blood,
A million a month in China are dying without
    God.

In September 1866 the *Lammermuir* limped into
Shanghai after a dreadful battering by a typhoon in the
South China Sea. Hudson Taylor and his team settled
in Hangchow where they set up a mission and began to
work, running a dispensary as well as establishing
outposts. Unfortunately one of the group, Lewis
Nichol, objected to wearing Chinese dress and, also,
to Hudson Taylor's familiarity with the ladies in the
group. He turned for support to George and Arthur
Moule, brothers and members of the C.M.S. in
Hangchow, who seemed to relish the tension thus set
up between the two missionary societies. As Maria
noted; 'one sometimes feels almost overwhelmed with
the sense of Satan's power here; but our God will not
forsake us.'

By the summer of the following year several more
recruits had arrived from England, and Hudson
Taylor, his family and several other pioneers moved
into the interior, some four hundred miles to Yangchow. Yangchow, described by the missionaries as a
'rich, proud and exclusive city . . . contained a
population of 360,000 souls still without any witness
for Christ.' The citizens were at first suspicious and

then hostile to the missionaries, and one hot summer afternoon a crowd of angry natives attacked the mission, shouting, 'Child-eaters', 'Kill them', 'Burn them'. The two wives, both pregnant, hid in an upper room with their frightened children. Windows and doors shattered; the crowd set fire to the house and the women had to jump to safety from a window to be caught by one of the missionaries below.

Amazingly none of the missionaries were seriously injured, but they had to leave the hostile city and move to the nearest town of Chingkiang where they awaited the first opportunity to return to Yangchow. This was not to be the end of the affair, however. British officials saw it as a flagrant violation of the rights of Her Majesty's subjects abroad; publicity escalated and soon the affair became a matter of importance for diplomats and even the House of Lords. Eventually four British gunboats steamed up the Yangtze River and threatened the city while the British minister in Peking opened negotiations. Although not wholly in support of the missionary endeavour – 'their doctrine is revolutionary . . . so why are they surprised if the ruling classes . . . oppose it with any means they can?' – he persuaded the Chinese to reach a settlement and a proclamation was issued to the people of Yangchow. It concluded, 'Anyone who disturbs the public mind will be arrested at once. Be serious! Obey with trembling!' So in November the missionaries returned to Yangchow in spite of criticism of their (as some saw it) reckless intrusion into unwelcoming foreign cities. As *The Times* put it; 'Parliament is not fond of missionaries, nor is the press, nor is general society.'

Hudson Taylor's vision had begun to take shape, however, and converts were made in Yangchow and elsewhere. By 1874 a hundred missionaries had been recruited by the China Inland Mission and were penetrating beyond Yangchow to even more remote areas. By this time, also, Maria Taylor had died after her eighth pregnancy at the age of thirty-three and Hudson Taylor had married another missionary, Jeannie Faulding, one of the original pioneers to leave England in *The Lammermuir* in 1866. Hudson Taylor, home on furlough, discovered his talent for publicity and stirred the emotions of thousands as he travelled England. His own gift for public speaking, added to the immensely popular revivalist meetings of Moody and Sankey which were attracting much publicity at the same time, eventually brought success: his prayerful appeals for more missionaries and more funds bore fruit when seven young Cambridge undergraduates volunteered to join the C.I.M.

The wave of enthusiasm for the missionary cause and particularly for the C.I.M., which 'The Cambridge Seven' had initiated, gained momentum and enabled Hudson Taylor to expand his missionary force. Gradually the C.I.M., nicknamed by the missionaries, 'Constantly in Motion', grew and spread throughout China to the province of Szectuan on the border of Tibet, until, by 1890, a total of 1,296 protestant missionaries were working in China, which claimed to have 37,287 Chinese communicants.

A missionary conference was held in Shanghai in May 1890 at which the now aged Hudson Taylor, still an indomitable presence, rose to reaffirm his society's aim to offer the gospel to all. 'This must be done', declared the old man, 'however difficult the task. It is the narrow way that leads to the Heavenly Country', he reminded his audience.

For many of his audience the way was to become bloody and terrifying; they were to be murdered by the Boxers – peasant revolutionaries who believed that their cult of boxing, a system of strenuous physical activity of Taoist origin, had endowed them with supernatural powers. Opposed to foreign presence in their country, they attacked the missionaries savagely, one day, in the province of Shansi, beheading forty-five foreigners whose heads were placed in cages on the gates of the city. But the rebellion was short-lived and its defeat marked a turning point in Chinese missionary history. The old gods and the old ways of the Boxers crumbled to be replaced by a more liberal regime. A more liberal interpretation of theological dogma matched this change of attitude; the social humanitarianism of christian teaching replaced, to a great extent, the image of missionaries as christian knights in armour in single-handed combat with heathendom.

To Hudson Taylor the new century must have seemed complex: his life had been dedicated to a single, simple belief; the saving of souls. He died with that faith still intact, aged seventy-three, in Hunan, having given his life for China. He had never deviated from that impassioned pledge made as a young man; 'If I had a thousand lives, China should have them. No! Not CHINA but CHRIST.'

THE CAMBRIDGE SEVEN
(1885–1946)

The Call to Duty

On a pouring wet evening in February 1885, in front of three and a half thousand people in Exeter Hall, London, a young man described his conversion thus: 'I had formerly as much love for cricket as any man could have, but when the Lord Jesus came into my heart I found that I had something infinitely better than cricket. My heart was no longer in the game. I wanted to win souls for the Lord. I knew that cricket would not last and nothing in the world would last, but it was worthwhile living for the world to come.'

The young man, Charles Studd, epitomized in the mind of his audience the emotive ideal of a gifted, handsome young man who had turned from worldly vanities to become a missionary. He stood in the public mind for an attitude of straightforward and social assurance and uncomplicated faith which gave the missionary vocation a heroic quality. From a privileged upper-class family, Charles Studd spent his schooldays at Eton where he distinguished himself as an excellent cricketer. Going up to Trinity College, Cambridge in 1879, he won his blue and played cricket for the University for four consecutive years, eventually achieving national fame when Cambridge University defeated the hitherto unbeaten Australians in 1882, when Charles scored a century. He went on, while still an undergraduate, to play in a test match against the Australians at the Oval. In the same year, Charles Studd was described by W.G. Grace, that most famous cricketer of the Victorian Age, as 'The most brilliant member of a well-known cricketing family . . . [he has] few superiors as an all-round player.'

By 1883 Charles Studd had become a household name, the idol of schoolboys and students. Yet he chose, along with six other Cambridge undergraduates, to give up worldly ambition and to follow Hudson Taylor to China as a member of the China Inland Mission. Their decision was inspired by the temper of the times they lived in; the gulf between the convictions of Charles Darwin, on the one hand, and the fervour of the Revivalist movement, led by the American Evangelists, Dwight Moody and Ira Sankey, on the other. To idealistic young people a choice had to be made between Darwin's scientific humanism, with its cold, honest rationality, and the emotive, fervent acceptance of Christ as preached by Moody and Sankey.

For many the appeal of Moody and Sankey was the more compelling. Dynamic central figures of the Revivalist movement, which had reached its peak in England in the 1870s, they travelled mainly to England's big industrial cities, erecting their two portable iron tabernacles, each capable of holding up to five thousand people, on the outskirts of the towns. Moody's earnest preaching, direct and compelling, was interspersed with Sankey's accompanying hymns, such as this favourite:

Hold the Fort for I am coming
    Jesus signals still;
Wave the answer back to Heaven,
    By Thy grace I will.

The vitality and spirit of active, confident Christianity awakened the consciences of those who felt a compelling need to give themselves whole-heartedly to a useful, worthy way of life. And of all those moved by Moody and Sankey, the group which most captured the public imagination were seven Cambridge undergraduates nicknamed 'The Cambridge Seven'.

One of The Seven, Dixon Hoste, a general's son, describes his first sight of the man who was to change his life like this, 'He was dressed in a business suit and had nothing of the customary clerical appearance about him. From the minute he stepped on the platform my eyes involuntarily followed his every movement. This was Mr Moody; there could be no mistake. There was something about him that was different.' Dixon came from a military family and, after attending school at Clifton College followed by training at the Royal Military Academy, he was already established in the army as a lieutenant in the Royal Artillery. His brother, William, who had been an undergraduate at Cambridge and had already been converted to Christianity by Moody and Sankey, persuaded his younger brother to attend a revivalist meeting given by the two American evangelists. Dixon, sitting at the back of the hall, became convinced as he listened to Moody that 'now is the accepted time, now is the time of salvation'. He returned to his post as lieutenant at the battery fort at Sandown in the Isle of Wight, but his thoughts returned constantly to his feelings at the meeting. 'It has changed my life, I want to make it known where Christ is not known. There are many people in other lands who have never heard it, and the Lord wants them to hear it for he says so. I want to give my life to this.' William kept him informed of the rising tide of missionary enthusiasm in Cambridge and sent him some literature about the China Inland Mission. Dixon wrote later; 'I became deeply impressed by the single-hearted, self-denying devotion to the cause of the Gospel in China, which characterized the writing of Hudson Taylor and others.' Above all, he was moved by Hudson Taylor's booklet *China's Spiritual Need and Claims*, which spoke of the millions of Chinese 'utterly and hopelessly beyond the reach of the gospel'. Hudson Taylor asked in the article, 'Can the Christians of England sit still with folded arms while these multitudes are perishing?' Dixon decided that he could not ignore what he felt to be a direct demand from a great missionary. His father gave him permission to resign his commission and Dixon wrote to Hudson Taylor in 1883, 'Sir, I have for some time been thinking about offering myself for the China Inland Mission. . .' He was interviewed by the elderly missionary and thus became the first of the seven to commit himself to China.

Three other members of The Seven had all progressed from school at Repton to Cambridge. Of these, only Montagu Beauchamp had any previous knowledge of Hudson Taylor and his missionary work. One of his earliest memories was, as a boy of five, Hudson Taylor's visit to his home, showing the Beauchamp children chopsticks and other Chinese curiosities. This visit had resulted in Sir Thomas' responding to Hudson Taylor's appeal for funds by giving him the insurance premium for his conservatories.

Monty Beauchamp's closest friend at Cambridge, Stanley Smith, was to prove to be the greatest orator of the seven and was later much admired at the missionary meetings, which were to stir the emotions of many. One onlooker described Stanley thus; 'All were moved by the sight of the big, muscular hands and long arms of the ex-captain of the Cambridge Eight, stretched out in entreaty while he told the old story of Redeeming Love. . .' Both he and Monty Beauchamp became converted to Christianity by another old Reptonian, the Honourable Granville Waldegrave. Stanley spent much of his vacations preaching and praying in the mission halls and open air of the London slums. However, although he kept up his open-air speaking in Hyde Park on Sundays, his time at Cambridge was mainly taken up with enthusiasm for rowing with a group of friends. Uncertain what to do with his future, Stanley felt he had been guided by God when he found the following text in the Bible which seemed to speak directly to him: 'I will also give thee for a light to the Gentiles, that thou mayest be my salvation unto the end of the earth' (Isaiah 6). Stanley was in no doubt; he had been called to become a missionary. God was sending him 'far hence to the Gentiles'. On 1 April 1884 he too was interviewed by Hudson Taylor and accepted as a probationer.

The third Repton man to become one of The Seven was William Cassels, a few years older than Beauchamp and Smith and, by the time they arrived at Cambridge, already having gained his degree at St

John's College was about to be ordained. He went on to become a curate in the parish of South Lambeth, worked in the Clapham Mission and found his interest focusing on missionary work in China.

Two brothers, Arthur and Cecil Polhill-Turner, completed The Seven. A traditional career pattern had been planned for them by their parents; while the eldest son, Frederick, would inherit, the second, Cecil, would enter the army and the youngest, Arthur, would be ordained and then take the family living. However, neither Arthur nor Cecil were to fulfil their parents' wish for them. Arthur, while at Trinity Hall, Cambridge, was another student to be moved by Moody and Sankey as they addressed a packed audience at the Corn Exchange. Moody spoke of the Prodigal Son and pictured the life led by so many of the people present, 'the hollow, drifting life with feeble, mundane ambitions – utterly selfish, giving no service, making no sacrifice, tasting the moment, gliding feebly down the stream of time to the roaring cataract of death'. Arthur, moved by a succession of revivalist meetings, decided that his life would have 'to be a good deal readjusted'. Consequently he joined Montagu Beauchamp, Charles Studd and others as an active member of the Cambridge Christian Union and gradually became convinced that, without waiting to complete his ordination, he should go as soon as possible as a missionary to China.

This conviction was influenced by Cecil's decision to give up his commission as second lieutenant in The Queen's Bays and go to China. Cecil, at first pointed in the direction of active Christianity by his younger brother, Arthur, quickly reached his decision to forfeit his future in the army. He joined Smith, Studd and Hoste who all felt an urgent need to follow in Hudson Taylor's footsteps. This sense of urgency helped Arthur to commit himself at the same time as his brother. He abandoned his training for ordination and joined at once in the 'Farewell' meetings arranged by Hudson Taylor, at which each of 'The Cambridge Seven' were called upon to explain their personal reasons for joining the China Inland Mission.

Ever since the announcement that Charles Studd was abandoning cricket at the height of his fame in favour of China, missionary fervour had swept the universities. Oxford undergraduates crowded to hear Studd and Smith in November 1884. 'My dear Mr Hudson Taylor' wrote Smith, after the first Oxford meeting, 'We were simply so full of joy of the Lord we could only wear the broadest grin on our faces for the rest of the night'. Cassels joined them and they swept on to Cambridge to be joined by the rest of The Seven and Hudson Taylor. Here, the sacrifice which the young men had decided to make captured the undergraduate imagination. As one student remarked afterwards; 'We have had missionary meetings and we have been hearing missionaries talk to us from time to time. But when men whom everyone has heard of and many known personally came up and said, "I am going out myself", we were brought face to face with the heathen abroad.'

The fame of The Seven spread not only among undergraduates but throughout the nation. It was the extent of their sacrifice which seemed so drastic. The young men were seen to be, as one speaker said,

'Putting aside the splendid prizes of earthly ambition which they might reasonably have expected to gain, taking leave of the social circles in which they shone with no mean brilliance and plunging into the warfare whose splendours are seen only by faith and whose rewards seem so shadowy to the unopened vision of ordinary men.' The Seven toured Britain – Newcastle, Manchester, Rochdale, Leeds, Aberdeen, Edinburgh – speaking to packed halls, giving their own testimonies and inviting their audience 'to consecrate themselves to the service of God', and wherever they went the atmosphere was charged with emotion. The climax came, of course, at the farewell meeting at Exeter Hall. 'Exeter Hall, last night. What shall I say? Such a meeting!' wrote one evangelist to Hudson Taylor. 'I question if a meeting of equal significance and spiritual fruitfulness has been held in that building during this generation. Its influence upon the cause of missions must be immense, incalculable.' Beneath a vast map of China were forty Cambridge undergraduates, all intending to be missionaries, and as The Seven filed in 'they were received', said *The Times*, 'with great enthusiasm' and each presented with a Chinese New Testament on behalf of the British and Foreign Bible Society, 'as a memento of this great occasion'. The hall resounded with the hymn, 'Tell it out among the Heathen that the Lord is King', then each of The Seven rose, for the last time in England, to tell their personal reasons for joining C.I.M. The evening finished on a climax of emotion and dedication with the hymn:

Take my love, my Lord, I pour
At thy feet its treasure store.
Take myself, and I will be
Ever, only, all for Thee.

Next morning admiring crowds gathered at Victoria Station to cheer The Seven on their way. The young men had come to epitomize muscular Christianity – manly, straightforward, socially assured and unquestioningly devout. As they sailed away to China they left in their wake a great wave of enthusiasm for the missionary cause. Over fifty thousand copies of a full report of the Exeter Hall meeting were printed and sold and, particularly in Edinburgh and Cambridge, groups of students spread out across the country holding revival meetings. At Cambridge Bishop Handley Moule was soon finding it 'constantly my duty at Ridley Hall to press urgently on men the claims of the homefield, so almost universal was the longing to serve the Lord in the end of the unevangelized world.'

'The Cambridge Seven' retained their buoyant spirits on arrival at Shanghai and re-invigorated the zeal of the more established missionaries there. They held a 'Meeting for the Deepening of the Spiritual Life' at Shanghai and then moved on to Peking where their impassioned speeches impressed many who felt that their coming was 'a salutary, purifying breeze'. At first their time in China had an ecstatic, highly charged quality; 'My all is on the Altar. The fire is come. He has given me a clean heart, Hallelujah!' ran one of Smith's first postcards home. 'It is a very honeymoon time with the Lord in a quiet, cool place', wrote Charles Studd. However, after being posted to various inland

71

mission stations the young men realized, as Hudson Taylor had done before them, that the attempt to Christianize China was not to be likened to a quick battle with 'the Evil One round about us as a roaring lion', but rather to a slow, lonely and pedestrian progress on a tiring journey.

Charles Studd and his wife Priscilla gave away all their inheritance, feeling that 'Henceforth our bank is in Heaven'. From then on they depended, as did their colleagues, on voluntary funding from well-wishers, though Charles Studd's family paid for the education of their four daughters. After some time posted at a remote village Charles' health broke down and he had to return to England in 1894, never to return to China. He felt compelled to continue as a missionary, however, and set off in 1910 for tropical Africa where he was instrumental in starting 'the Heart of Africa' Mission and the Worldwide Evangelization Crusade. Charles Studd died at Ibambi, Belgian Congo, in 1931, a splendid figure to the end.

Stanley Smith also died in 1931 after a lifetime spent in Northern China. He became a fine linguist and as fluent a preacher in Chinese as in English. In 1902 he left the C.I.M. because he disagreed with certain fundamental beliefs which his colleagues held, and from then on worked as an independent missionary in Eastern Shansi.

William Cassels was the first of The Seven to open his own mission station. He was allotted by Hudson Taylor the province of Szechwan, an enormous area stretching westwards to the Tibetan frontier and with a population of some sixty-eight million. Cassels saw his work there as being 'to build up a work . . . within the C.I.M. that is loyal and consistent with Church of

England principles' and he devoted his life to it. He spent a total of thirty-eight years in Szechwan and died there in 1925, still 'girt in full armour in the midst of his grand work' as Cecil Polhill-Turner put it.

Cecil Polhill (the brothers dropped the 'Turner' part of their name), became intent on reaching Tibet and settled there in Kansu with his wife. Moving south to Sungpan in Western Szechwan, still bordering Tibet, they almost lost their lives in a violent riot in 1892. Eventually withdrawn in 1900 to the coast because of the Boxer Rising, Cecil Polhill was invalided home and forbidden by his doctor to return to China. He inherited the family home and died there in 1938, aged eighty.

His brother, Arthur, was ordained in China in 1888 and lived in Northern Szechwan, travelling throughout that province and surviving both the Boxer Rising and the Revolution of 1911. In 1928 at the age of sixty-six he retired and took a country living in Hertfordshire, where he died in 1935.

Monty Beauchamp, the itinerant member of The Seven, loved travelling and once accompanied Hudson Taylor 'about a thousand miles in intense heat, walking through market towns and villages, living in Chinese inns and preaching the Gospel to crowds day by day.' He always carried either a scroll or a large palm leaf fan attached to a stick, inscribed, 'Repent, the Kingdom of Heaven is at Hand'. Evacuated in the Boxer Rising of 1900, Beauchamp was again in China from 1902–1911. He then returned to England and was ordained, becoming a chaplain to the forces in the First World War and serving in Egypt, Greece and Russia. He had inherited the baronetcy when his elder brother was killed at Gallipoli on the same day as his own eldest son. After the war he continued to visit China and in 1939, aged seventy-nine, he joined a party of missionary recruits driving overland through French Indo-China via Hanoi to Chunking; but he was suffering from cancer and died at his second son's mission station, Paoning, in October 1939.

The last of The Seven to die was also the first who had offered himself to China. Dixon Hoste worked in Sansi until 1896 and then succeeded Hudson Taylor as head of the C.I.M. in 1903, leading the mission for thirty years. He remained in Shanghai at the outbreak of the Second World War and was interned by the Japanese, leaving China in 1945, weak and ill. He died in London in May 1946.

The story of 'The Cambridge Seven' is the story of ordinary men who, because of their social background and religious zeal, caught the imagination of Victorian England. Certainly not without fault, over-exuberance of word and action being, perhaps, the most obvious, they illustrated whole-hearted commitment to their belief; a response to what they felt to be the call of God and a consecration of their lives to his service.

GLADYS AYLWARD

(1902–1970)

The Small Woman

One evening in November 1932, a small young woman with dark hair tied neatly in a bun, stood on the deck of the Japanese ship and stared across the muddy sea. Behind the dark landfall ahead the sun set with a flamboyant display of colour. The woman was Gladys Aylward and the approaching land was China. At last Gladys had arrived at her longed-for destination.

The desire to go to China had arisen during the time that Gladys had been a parlour-maid in London and had once, out of curiosity, attended a religious revival meeting. Here she came to feel, suddenly, that the exhortation to serve God was directed at her and that she must obey. This conviction never left her. She joined a local evangelical society and one day read in a newspaper about the great nation of China which was opening its doors, at last, to western civilization. Gladys was seized with the conviction that God wanted her to live and work in this far-off country and to teach the people about Christ. She decided to enrol as a probationer missionary at the China Mission Centre and did so in 1930, but her hopes were soon shattered when she found herself unable to pass the necessary examinations. To her bitter disappointment she was asked to leave as soon as her probationary period had expired, and was sent to work as a parlour-maid again, this time for two retired mission-aries in Bristol. From this post she volunteered to be a 'Rescue Sister' on the Swansea Docks, patrolling the area night after night, endeavouring to persuade women to abandon their life as prostitutes and to seek shelter in the mission hostel. Gladys' work in Swansea strengthened her spiritual resolve but did not help her dreams of China to fade. She decided to return for a third time to the life of a parlour-maid in order to finance the passage to China for herself.

And so it was that Gladys returned again to London, this time in the service of Sir Francis Younghusband, an eminent soldier, author and explorer. Ironically, this little woman dusting books in the library of the great explorer who had crosssed the heart of Central Asia by traversing the great mountain barrier between Kashmir and China was herself to cross terrain as formidable as any he had faced. Yet, for the moment, any idea of even reaching China must have seemed remote to the thirty year-old parlour-maid as she sat on the edge of her narrow servant's bed, holding her bible and her first savings and praying with passionate earnestness; 'Oh God! Here's my Bible, here's my money! Use us, God! Use us!'

Hope, though difficult to maintain, never ebbed away. Instead, Gladys never deviated from her resolve and by working night and day – weekends and days-off included – she eventually managed to save enough money to buy a ticket to China by the cheapest means available – a seat on the Trans-Siberian railway. Not only was the transport now an actuality, but Gladys had also found someone to work for when she arrived in China – an elderly missionary called Mrs Lawson who had written and asked for Gladys' help. At last, on Saturday 18 October 1932, the parlour-maid who had never travelled further than the Isle of Wight, waved goodbye to her family and friends and boarded the train, carrying her two suitcases and wearing a corset whose pockets contained her passport, fountain pen, some traveller's cheques and a small bible.

The journey was not uneventful; war between China and Russia over possession of the China Eastern Railway halted the train in Siberia and Gladys had to walk back down the line, over the icy tracks, to the nearest station. Mistaken at first for an English communist eager to offer her services to Russia, she eventually managed to disillusion officials of the belief that this was her aim. She travelled slowly through Siberia, unable to speak the language, having to change trains frequently; utterly alone. Misunderstood and in danger of never reaching China, she was miraculously smuggled from Vladivostock to a Japanese ship by an unknown Russian girl who had noticed that Gladys was in trouble. She sailed away from Russia with much thankfulness and landed in Japan instead of China with no regrets; 'It seems like heaven after the desolateness of Russia', she wrote home. After a rest there she sailed to Tientsin in China and from there was conducted on the last stage of her incredible journey; first a month's trek with a Chinese guide to the city of Tsehchow in the Shansi Province where Gladys had been told she would find Mrs Lawson; then a rough journey on mule-back through mountainous, wild, bandit-infested country to find the old lady. At last they found the town of Yangcheng built high on a mountain, delicate pagodas growing, it seemed, from the natural rock and rising above the city wall. Out of the dilapidated mission buildings stepped an old lady dressed in a tunic and trousers; 'Well, and who are you?' she inquired abruptly. Thus began an odd friendship between the naive, affectionate, eager Gladys and the irascible old Scottish missionary, toughened by a lifetime in China. Together they shared the life of outcasts or 'foreign devils' in Yangcheng, which had never before seen missionaries and treated them with suspicion mixed with fear. Eventually, Jeannie Lawson conceived the idea of turning the mission station into an inn and calling it the 'Inn of the Eighth Happiness'. Here, she thought, she and Gladys would provide food and rest for travellers and have the additional opportunity to tell them the stories of Jesus. Gladys was given the task of persuading the muleteers to choose their inn; 'No fleas, no bugs! Good! Good! Come! Come!' she would shout, standing on the mountain trail, pulling on the mules bridles to urge them to turn in. And so they did, for a while, and the inn became a popular resting place. Jeannie Lawson's temper, though, was both unreasonable and unpredictable. Turning on Gladys one day she demanded that she leave immediately. Gladys, though not knowing what she had done wrong, could not pacify the old lady and so, to give Jeannie time to reconsider, she left and returned to Tsehchow. Only three days later a messenger arrived with the news that Jeannie was dying; she had slipped and fallen from a balcony onto the ground beneath.

The death of Jeannie Lawson left Gladys totally alone at the Inn of the Eighth Happiness with only a friendly Chinese cook for company. At this time a most unlikely person entered her life; someone who would initiate her into the mysteries of China as no one else could. One day a procession arrived at the inn; coolies bore a curtained sedan chair around which walked men in robes of dark blue – the Mandarin's clerks and retainers. From the chair stepped a picture from an almost bygone, feudal age; a man with a fine thin face, round silk cap and embroidered gown – the Mandarin of Shansi. He came with a strange request. The central government had ordered that the custom of binding womens' feet should stop immediately and the Mandarin needed a woman with unbound feet to undertake the work of inspection. Gladys undertook the work on the understanding that she would try to convert the people she came into contact with to Christianity. Thus the unknown missionary became part of China's feudal system, 'The Mandarin's personal foot inspector'. Her position gave her a certain amount of respect in the eyes of the Chinese and, as well as this, she acquired the means to travel to distant villages, ostensibly to inspect feet but also to absorb Chinese customs, dialect and attitudes. Gladys fell in love with China; the lonely, beautiful country, and the urban Mandarin who, as his friendship and admiration for the missionary developed, explained the ancient culture of the country to her. It was he who christened Gladys *Ai-weh-deh*, which means, 'the virtuous one', and it was by this name that she was known for all her remaining years in China. It was during this peaceful period that Gladys adopted her first child, a starving little girl sold by her mother to Gladys for ninepence. 'Ninepence', as the little girl was nicknamed, came to live at the inn, followed soon by a succession of destitute and starving children who had been abandoned or orphaned, until before long, Gladys was unofficial mother to five children.

The richly rewarding years sped by. Gladys grew to feel that the Chinese were her people and she became a naturalized Chinese in 1936. She came to be loved and respected by the people because, as one of her Chinese friends wrote, she was unlike conventional missionaries who 'come to China not purely for preaching the Gospel . . . most of them are very comfortable, and therefore very few people in China believe Jesus Christ. Because the people see that it is not same what is saying in The Bible when they have it compared.'

Gladys lived her life according to the Bible, in good times and in bad. The bad time came suddenly one spring morning in 1938, when pretty little silver planes swooped down over the mountains bringing with them an endless prospect of war. It was the Japanese, who ruthlessly bombed Yangcheng before sweeping off to attack Tsehchow; later they would return to destroy what was left of the wrecked town. Gladys and the Mandarin decided to evacuate before this happened and moved in separate parties, taking the townsfolk to tiny hamlets high up in the mountains where they hoped they would never be discovered.

So began many months of fugitive living, hiding in small christian communities, living in caves, visiting the sacked town of Yangcheng at night to bury the dead and to remove the wounded. It was during this terrifying time that Gladys wrote home; 'Do not wish me out of this or in any way seek to get me out, for I will not be got out while this trial is on. These are my people; God has given them to me, and I will live or die with them for Him and His Glory.'

The Japanese raids became more frequent and Gladys and her followers soon learned of the brutality of the soldiers. Many friends suffered, were tortured and had families killed before their eyes. Life was constant tension. Gladys, although initially believing that the role of a Christian was one of neutrality, gradually came to feel that she must support the Chinese Nationalists in their battle against the Japanese; her love of China was so great and the sufferings of those around her so appalling. She met 'General' Ley, a young Dutch roman catholic priest from a mission in southern Shansi who had made a similar decision; he trained and led guerillas against the enemy. She made journeys behind enemy lines to gather information for the Chinese armies. Eventually she discovered that the Japanese had offered a reward of one hundred dollars for 'information leading to the capture, alive, of the Small Woman, known as *Ai-Wei-Deh*.'

Incredulity at her own notoriety was replaced by well-founded fear. Gladys opened her bible and the page spoke to her; 'Flee ye, flee ye into the mountains; dwell deeply in hidden places, because the King of Babylon has conceived a purpose against you' she read. God had spoken: she must escape. She remembered hearing that Madame Chiang-Kei-shek had started a fund for war orphans and that the children were collected from war-ravaged areas and sent to the ancient capital of Sian in Shensi, and there fed, clothed and sheltered. She quickly decided to take destitute children from the dangerous areas of Tsehchow and Yangcheng and

81

embark at once on the perilous journey. Collecting as many children as possible from the mission at Tsehchow she returned along the rocky track to Yangcheng. For the last time she spoke to the old Mandarin who blessed her and gave all he could – millet to provide food for part of the journey and two men to carry it.

At dawn the next morning, Gladys and nearly a hundred children left the broken Inn of the Eighth Happiness for ever and marched out of the wrecked town of Yangcheng towards the mountains, each carrying a bowl, chopsticks and a quilt for bedding. Gladys was now responsible for a *bei* – the Chinese for a hundred – children aged from fifteen to four; most of them wild, undisciplined and unaware of the danger they faced: among the *bei* was the eight year-old *Ninepence* and the other original members of the Aylward family. At first excitement made the going easy, but by the end of a week the hot sun and the unfamiliar territory and lack of sleep made constant walking increasingly exhausting. The mountain stretched ahead of them, wild and barren and so steep that they often had to form a human chain down the mountainside to pass the younger children from hand to hand. Food was running out; they were constantly thirsty. Once a contingent of Chinese Nationals came across them and gave them food, at other times villages took them in. And so the march continued. At last they descended from the mountains towards the Yellow River, believing that having crossed this they would be safe from the Japanese.

But they had arrived too late: the town which lay by the side of the river was deserted, the ferry

82

destroyed. The local people had fled, hearing of the approach of the Japanese. For three days Gladys and her children camped by the banks of the great, swirling river, praying that God would allow them to cross. Amazingly, they were discovered starving, dirty and despairing by a platoon of Chinese Nationalists who ferried them across but still they were not safe from the approaching enemy. Kindly officials allowed them onto a refugee train which took them part of the still very long way to Sian, but an important bridge had been blown up and the railway line destroyed and so, after a few days on the train, the refugees had to disembark and march once more towards another range of high mountains. Over these waited the refuge of Sian, many miles away.

Following the long, straggling trail, Gladys and her band of children moved up through the rocky passes. Progress was slow: Gladys was feeling very ill by this time; some of the young children needed constant carrying; they were all nearing the end of their resources. But as usual, villagers gave food and rest and eventually the mountains were behind them and they were able to beg another lift by another train, to Sian.

At last, after a month's travelling, they arrived to find the great walled city full of refugees: the gates were closed and they were not allowed in. For so long they had believed in the mirage of Sian only to find it shattered. Now they had nothing to sustain them except a temporary refugee camp set up outside the city walls. Then news came of an orphanage and school at Fufeng, not many days journey away by train. And it was here, at Fufeng, that they at last found refuge, were given clean clothes and new shoes, allotted places to sleep and generally rehabilitated. It was here too that Gladys collapsed one day as she was about to preach a sermon, gravely ill with typhus fever and pneumonia.

So ended the heroic trek from Yangcheng. Gladys' life was saved but she seemed to have lost her driving force. For a long time afterwards she suffered from periods of confusion and wandered the streets of Fufeng not knowing who she was or why she was there. Then gradually, physical and mental health returned and her children were sent away to school. Ninepence married and Gladys went to work at an American Mission in western Szechwan, almost on the borders of Tibet. Later she recalled that this time was the most demoralizing and lonely for her; certainly some words written in the margin of her Chinese bible in 1944 testify to her feelings:

Lonely! The very word can start the tears. . .
Who walk with Christ can never walk alone.
Alone, but not alone. He is here. G.A.

The years in Szechuan nearly broke her heart for the old China was breaking up. Still at war with Japan, the ancient country now had another enemy, the communists. To them, Gladys and her missionary colleagues were evil, and Gladys saw many of her fellows maltreated, persecuted and forced to leave China. Even more heartrendingly, she wrote later, 'I watched my boys die, to be taken away to concentration camps, or to prison. Less, [one of her adopted boys], was to die, shot by the Reds when, as a student, he refused to do something which was contrary to his Christian beliefs. . .'

84

At this time of near despair, one American mission gave Gladys the money for her fare back to England. After seventeen years away, she was met from the station in 1949 by her parents, who did not at first recognise the bewildered little Chinese woman. After some time at home a journalist, named Alan Burgess, discovered her living in London and, realizing that he had struck journalistic oil, dramatized her story on the BBC and followed this up with the book, *The Small Woman*. She began to be known, travelling throughout Britain, telling her story to enthusiastic audiences. She also helped to befriend lonely Chinese refugees who had begun to arrive in London. From them and from friends remaining in China she realized that she would never be able to return to the country she loved. The communists had gained control and suspected her of being a spy for the Imperialists: if she went back she would be murdered.

The book *The Small Woman* became a bestseller and Gladys a celebrity. However, all that this meant to Gladys was that she had enough money to return to the Far East. If she could not return to China, she would be welcome in Hong Kong. So in April 1957 she sailed from England and went to help the destitute refugees from Communism who were flooding across the border between China and Hong Kong. She could not remain permanently and in the autumn of 1957 she went on to Taiwan where she remained for the last thirteen years of her life. Here she continued her missionary work, preaching and once again running an orphanage at her home in Taipei. To raise money she would often travel abroad, especially to America, to give talks about her experiences, her diminutive appearance – about five feet high with two black plaits tied round her head and wearing a Chinese gown – was slightly unusual: the tales she told were extraordinary.

The end came suddenly one damp, chilly day at the beginning of 1970 when Gladys, at home in Taipei, succumbed again to pneumonia and died peacefully in the night. To the end of her life she had lived by one of her own maxims written in the margin of her Chinese bible; 'The eagle that soars in the upper air does not worry itself how it is to cross rivers.'

THE PENTECOSTAL MARTYRS

(1978)

'With love in Jesus'

The work of the Elim Pentecostal Church began in Rhodesia, as Zimbabwe was then called, in 1946 when Dr Cecil Brian and his wife began their mission work in a tent, pitched by a stream in the bush at Caterere. They felt they had been guided by God to go out into the deep country where no missionaries had ever been before, and where there were no schools or hospitals and no knowledge of Jesus Christ. Twenty-five years later the fruits of their brave adventure into the unknown were considerable; a one hundred bed hospital in Caterere, now a town of about a thousand inhabitants centered round the mission; a school with two hundred and eighty boarders, and a church with numerous small chapels scattered throughout the bush associated with it. The elim pentecostals continued to draw people to work at their thriving mission.

It was this place near the Mozambique border that, in the early 1970s attracted a group of missionaries, among whom were fourteen all to be massacred one night in June 1978. All members of the Elim Pentecostal Church, they made up a cross-section of society. There was Roy Lynn, a Northern Irishman from a farming family who was an expert mechanic and used the skills of his trade in the mission. Whilst at Caterere he had married the hospital matron, Joyce Pickering, a Yorkshire woman, and by 1978 they had a three-week-old baby called Pamela.

Another missionary family were the Evans, Phillip, Sue and their three children. They had, as Sue put it, 'made our lives available to God' and feeling that 'he wants to use them now', had left their home in Nuneaton where Philip had been a schoolteacher and had moved to Caterere. Other members of the group were two young single women; Mary Fisher, who used to sing at services and accompany herself on the guitar and Wendy White, a nurse, teacher and social worker who had newly arrived at the mission. A third, older woman, Catherine Picken, who had served in the Congo and another teacher, Peter McCann, who taught science at the Elim Secondary School, his wife Sandra and their baby girl, Lynn, made up the fourteen.

By the time this little group had arrived in Caterere the Rhodesian Civil War had been going on a long time, continually intensifying, particularly following the declaration of Unilateral Independence, into a conflict which came to involve the whole country. The bush areas were particularly vulnerable to attack, for it was here that guerrillas – 'the boys in the bush' as they came to be called – were a permanent background terror, suddenly striking white farmers or African villagers indiscriminately. Roads were mined, farms raided, cattle killed, villagers intimidated and their young people sometimes kidnapped and taken to join the insurgent forces over the border in Mozambique, or elsewhere. The prolonged fear and fighting was a high price to pay for independent Zimbabwe which was the end result.

The good intentions, selflessness and neutrality of missionaries in Zimbabwe at this critical time, made them easy prey to attack. As Phillip Evans testified, they wanted to be on no side but God's; 'We don't preach politics in this mission, we preach Jesus Christ and his love for us all – black and white. He died for us all, then rose again, and he is alive today. That's what we preach here.' But to the revolutionary Freedom Fighters seeking independence the white missionaries constituted 'the enemy'.

Twenty missionaries had been killed before that June night of 1978. In December of 1976 a Roman Catholic bishop, a priest and two nuns were held up as they were travelling by car and all except one murdered. A Swiss Roman Catholic priest, cycling on his way to preach at a church, vanished without trace. In February 1977 eight Roman Catholic mission-workers, including four nuns, were shot dead. Later a minister of the Dutch Reformed Church, together with his wife, died in an ambush. Another Roman Catholic priest, last seen riding his motor cycle near the capital, Salisbury, was apparently abducted and murdered. Two other Catholic missionaries, a German and a Swiss, were killed at a mission school close to the Botswana border and two young Salvation Army women officers were gunned down when the army Usher Institute was raided twenty miles from Bulawayo.

With this background of bloody and violent killings the small group at Caterere had good reason to feel apprehensive, but loving their work and caring for the people of the mission came first. In fact, as the war intensified, so their commitment to their vocation increased. Now, after landmines had exploded around

Caterere, the missionaries would have to travel around after the incidents, collecting victims and bringing them back to be nursed in the mission hospital. They provided a centre of peace in a war-torn community.

One night their own lives were threatened for the first time. It was April 1976 and Sue and Phillip Evans had staying with them a visitor, Joan Caudell, also on the staff of the Elim Secondary School at Caterere. Several other members of the mission staff were away that night and the place was unusually silent. The Evans may have felt apprehensive; there had recently been rumours of an incident at a catholic mission not far away where a group of terrorists had gone by night and spoken in a threatening manner. The children in bed, the three friends sat together listening to the radio. A sudden banging on their door startled them and when Phillip Evans went to the hallway he could see through the mesh screen the faces of three men in battle dress. With them was one of the African teachers at the school who said, in a frightened voice, that the men wanted to talk. Without opening the door Phillip spoke to them through a window, explaining that he and his family were missionaries and not involved with politics. To this one of the men replied, 'I used to believe what you believe . . . I prayed that God would liberate us Africans, but he didn't answer. So now I trust in this!' He indicated his gun. The guerrillas then asked for medicines and food and after receiving these supplies they left, threatening that if any of the missionaries contacted the Security Forces they would come back and shoot them.

The terror of the night was not yet over. Another member of staff, Joy Bath, was woken by her dog barking. Again, an African teacher from the school appeared at the door and again announced that 'some visitors' wanted to see her. It was the same group of guerrillas who had brought Joyce Pickering, the matron, with them from her house. Again they demanded drugs and food and proclaimed themselves to be Freedom Fighters. Joy Bath's parents, staying with their daughter, heard the disturbance. Creeping out of bed they stood hand in hand listening and praying. When the guerrillas had gone the group read together from the Bible. They looked up 'fear' in the index and were referred to Psalm 91; 'He who dwells in the shelter of the most high, who abides in the shadow of the Almighty, you will say to the Lord, "My refuge and my fortress; my God, in whom I trust . . . You will not fear the terror of the night." '

After several months of tension the elim authorities decided to move the mission out of Caterere away from the border to what was considered a safer area. This was a difficult move; the group of missionaries had grown to love Caterere. It was a beautiful place in a beautiful country and it was their home. However, the safety of their families and their mission depended upon their moving into the buildings of *The Eagle*, a preparatory school for European boys thirty miles from the town of Umtali. 'The Emergency', as the prolonged fight for independence was called, had emptied the school and the mission had to pack themselves into the small building.

Still they were not safe. Political and military conditions worsened and areas nearer the town became as vulnerable to violence as country areas.

Once again the missionary group were advised to move, this time to find themselves accommodation in the town of Umtali and sleep there, going out to the school to teach only by day. The missionaries made their own arrangements and began to pack, regretting the necessity for constant upheaval, yet prepared to accept the difficult situation.

On the night of 23 June 1978 the little group prepared to pack for the last time. Wendy, one of the single girls, was writing to a friend and ended the letter, 'with much love in Jesus, Wendy.' She was to die a week later in a Salisbury hospital, the only one of the group to survive the night. Unknown to them, a group of guerrillas had rounded up the African pupils and staff of the school and forced them to stay silent within their houses until dawn. The guerrillas were then free to creep stealthily up to the mission-ary houses, capture them and take them with their children out into the bush where they were slain.

The massacre was reported with blunt poignancy by one newspaper: 'I arrived at the scene three hours after the corpses were discovered. Here on a grassy bank sheltered by acacia trees lay three family groups and their close friends. All had died an agonizing death.' He went on to describe how nearby there was a blackboard still bearing the score from the last game of cricket and alongside, the body of an elderly woman – Catherine Picken – with her hair in pink and white plastic curlers. A young woman in a blue jersey lay spreadeagled nearby – Joyce Pickering – hand out-stretched towards a week old baby. Other bodies lay near; a man in a check shirt, three small children and a young woman who lay unconscious but alive in the long grass. All had been beaten and killed with clubs and axes.

The only first-hand account of the massacre comes from a member of the guerrilla party responsible for the killings who, weeks afterwards, was shot by the security forces. A notebook found in his pocket contained an entry which read: 'On Friday, 23 June 1978 is the day and the date we reached Ngue mission on the Vumba area near Matondo Camp in Zimunya District. Time of operation from 6.30–9pm . . . Total number of comrades who were there 21 . . . Weapons used, axes and knobkerries. Aim: to destroy the enemies. We killed 12 whites, including four babies.'

The massacre caused an international feeling of pity and shock. The brutality of the killings, contrasted with the simple trust of the missionaries who had, literally, given their lives to God, gave the scene of the massacre the quality of a vivid tableau of slain innocents. But perhaps the group of elim pentecostal missionaries had not given their lives in vain. As an African who had been a pupil at the school wrote after the event; 'The world will see that killing one Christian is actually multiplying us. The blood of the Christian martyrs is the seed for new Christians. In this way the Church will triumph when it is oppressed and progress when it is despised. Now I believe that it is my duty to spread the Gospel.'

PAUL BRAND

(1914–   )

Surgeon to the Lepers

When Krishnamurthy arrived at the surgery in Vellore he displayed all the worst foot and hand disabilities of leprosy. There were enormous foul smelling ulcers on the soles of both feet, so deeply infected that the bones lay exposed. His hands were wasted and useless, each finger curled into the clawed position, completely unable to grasp any object except by a pathetic attempt to pinch between the thumb and the side of the index finger. Krishnamurthy's mental condition had been flawed as much as his body. A well-educated man from a wealthy family, he had a bright future before him until the first tell-tale signs of leprosy appeared. When the disease was diagnosed the family had turned him out; he had lost his job and, abandoning all hope, had withdrawn into a cringing beggar-like state.

This man, Paul Brand's first leprosy patient, presented both physical and psychological deformities which appeared extremely daunting. Yet Paul Brand took on the challenge. 'Would you be willing', he asked Krishnamurthy, 'to let me do some operations on your hands and feet?' A shrug was all the answer Brand received. He began by examining the patient's feet drooping with paralysis and covered with the scars of partly-healed ulcers. Brand's idea was to take a tendon

94

from a paralysed muscle and attach one end of it to the side of the foot and the other to the fibula bone of the leg so that it held up the foot, thus allowing more movement and, consequently, less ulceration.

The operation, crude though it was, proved successful. Now Brand turned to Krishnamurthy's hands. Surely the paralysis of muscles which caused the claw could be overcome by transplanting good muscles in their stead. So taking muscles which could be spared, in this case the muscle which bends the second joint of each finger, Brand began a series of long, intricate operations on Krishnamurthy's hands. During the months of operations and intensive physiotherapy the claws transformed themselves gradually back into hands until the patient could open and shut them with almost normal action. The recreation of the man was even more rewarding; Krishnamurthy regained his confidence and lively intelligence. Curious about Paul and the other hospital staff who had given him the use of 'new' hands and feet, he learnt from them the christian faith, was baptised and chose to take a new name, John. After a year in hospital he was discharged, ready to start a new life.

Yet in two months he was back almost as despondent as before. 'These are not good hands . . . they are bad BEGGING hands', explained Krishnamurthy despondently. Because he still bore the stigmata of leprosy – the collapsed nose and lack of eyebrows – nobody would employ him or give him a place to live. Before, seeing his useless hands, people had taken pity and thrown him coins, but now that his hands were cured they showed no compassion. Brand questioned himself. If he continued to cure lepers as he had cured Krishnamurthy, would he be merely refashioning lepers with no capacity to beg? He realized that his patients must have their lives refashioned as well as their bodies; they must be taught new means of livelihood, trades which they could pursue without depending on employment. This meant trained, skilled instructors to teach them as well as physiotherapists to watch the movements of the limbs at work and to decide what trades were most suitable for them. The idea of a rehabilitation community for lepers came gradually to Brand and, prompted by donations from a few friends, the *Nava Jeeva Nilayam* or 'New Life Centre' was created.

Paul Brand the missionary-surgeon had always wanted to follow in the footsteps of his parents, both missionaries in India. His parents had dedicated themselves totally to the people of India and, stationed in a village high in the Kolli Malai mountains near Madras, acted as teachers, doctors, preachers, naturalists and agriculturalists to the people they had come to live amongst. Here Paul and his sister Connie were born and passed their childhood until they were sent back to England to complete their education. While at University College School, Paul met a builder who recognised the boy's skill at handling wood and tools. Realizing that the practical craft of building would be extremely useful to a missionary, Paul left school at the age of sixteen and became a builder's apprentice. He spent five years travelling from the genteel world of St John's Wood, where he lodged with his aunts and Connie, across London to the East End where he learnt his trade. At the same time he began to preach and became involved in youth work, helping to start a 'Fellowship of Youth', which included young people from all over London.

Perhaps it was the early death of his father from fever, and the need of his indomitable mother to continue her missionary work in the Kolli Mountains with a companion, which prompted the young Paul to follow so nearly in his father's footsteps. His father had been in the building trade until he left to become a missionary. He had taken a course in tropical medicine. So Paul decided, would he.

He enrolled at the Livingstone Medical School for a year's intensive course and at the end of that time his aptitude for medical work had been noticed and he was advised to train to become a doctor. At first he rejected this idea; having spent so many years studying he felt it was time to stop preparing and start acting. Consequently he enrolled in a missionary training colony in the summer of 1936. Brand soon felt he had made a mistake; merely preaching and trying to convert people was not enough he felt; he needed to be able to help people in a practical way. And so he left the colony and, in 1937 entered University College Medical School.

He found his studies extremely difficult at first as he had no knowledge of basic science. However his natural aptitude and ability to work hard made up for initial gaps of knowledge and he became an excellent medical student. During his medical training, two momentous events occurred: Brand fell in love and married a very gifted medical student contemporary, Margaret Berry; and the Second World War brought the blitz to London. There was bombing around the hospital nearly every night. It was organized into a casualty clearing station with medical students working on a full duty basis as part of the hospital team, studying by day and helping with the crowds of wounded who were brought in at night.

By 1943 both Paul and Margaret Brand had qualified as doctors. Paul continued his work as a house surgeon at University College Hospital and began to study for the F.R.C.S. examination at the same time. Although he had little time to study he was one of the eleven out of more than one hundred aspirants to pass the difficult primary examination. The following year there was even less time for study as Brand became surgical officer at Great Ormond Street Hospital for Sick Children. The war continued, bombings by day and night transforming London into one vast holocaust. During one of these nights, Paul and Margaret's first child was born and when Paul returned from fire-watching on top of the eight storey hospital he found a telegram on his table; 'To inform you that you are the father of a bonny, bouncing boy'.

The war ended at last. Brand, by now an assistant of the surgical unit of University College Hospital, qualified for his F.R.C.S. Because of staff shortages due to the war he was operating almost constantly and had no time to consider his future. Suddenly the telegram arrived; 'There is an urgent need for a surgeon to teach at Vellore. Can you come immediately on short term contract? (Signed) Cochrane.' Dr Robert Cochrane, the foremost leprosy specialist in the world had heard of Paul through Evelyn Brand, Paul's mother. This dynamic and forceful man had expanded the Vellore Medical College and Hospital from a small dispensary into a hospital complex with branches which, together, cared annually for a hundred thousand patients. Brand was persuaded to leave his wife behind in England since she was expecting their second child, and journeyed again to India, returning after an absence of twenty-three years.

Paul's first visit to the leper's sanatorium shocked him. The hospital inmates were everywhere, stumping along on bandaged feet, staring with empty, blind eyes. But his professional curiosity superceded shock as he examined for the first time a leprosy patient's hands. No one had attempted to discover the means of correcting the hideous deformities of leprosy he realized and the reason for this was obvious. Leprosy had for so long been a disease associated with outcasts from the human race; its cruel disfigurements repelling, and its legacy of contagion scaring away even doctors. Yet leprosy was less contagious than tuberculosis and adults were relatively insusceptible. Brand, trained in orthopaedic surgery, felt compelled to discover ways of repairing the ravages of leprosy.

His research took him to village sanatoria around Vellore where he and his team tested for that classic symptom of leprosy, loss of sensation, measured the movements of fingers and feet and discovered which muscles were paralysed. Brand discovered that the order in which muscles became paralysed was always the same and because of this it was possible to predict which muscles would never be affected even if the disease progressed. He knew, therefore, that there were 'good' muscles to take the place of those paralysed. It was possible to operate.

After his success with his first patient, Krishna-murthy, and the opening of the 'New Life Centre',

Paul and Margaret – who had by now joined him with their two children – knew that their lives were from now on to be dedicated to the repairing of lepers' damaged bodies and minds. Brand began by teaching patients such as Krishnamurthy a trade which would make them self-sufficient, and as he did most of the teaching himself at first, he introduced skills connected with his own carpenter's training. He instructed them in the use of tools and taught them how to make toys – jigsaws, cars and toy animals. These were all carefully sterilized and sold; the very act of selling breaking down some of the prejudice.

As the Centre became established so a team of people evolved to help Brand – a rare fellowship of dedicated persons. But perhaps the most valuable members of the team were not the social workers, doctors, nurses, or physiotherapists, but the patients themselves, all involved in eradicating their common enemy – leprosy. It was they who helped Brand discover that loss of sensation in limbs once affected by leprosy was as much responsible for loss of fingers and toes as the actual disease itself. Not only could fingers and toes become damaged by tools with sharp cutting edges without the patients' knowledge, but lack of sensation led to bizarre loss of fingers at night, traced to rats who feasted on patients' bodies as they lay asleep. Brand, as he said during a lecture, realized that 'once pain is lost, different parts of the body may revert to competition with each other. Thus our very survival depends on pain.'

Unconscious destruction of the human body because of the absence of pain, as seen in the case of lepers, became basic to Brand's understanding of human nature, and he extended the living evidence of absence of pain into his philosophy of life; 'In human society we are suffering because we do not suffer enough . . . with the acceptance of the discipline of pain, suffering for one another, will come also the ecstasy of shared happiness and of new understanding as we glimpse the vision of God for pain.'

Many experiments and successes with leprous hands and feet brought Paul more and more patients. And yet the other stigmata prevented once-leprous patients from returning to a normal life. The passionate desire of leprosy patients for a normal appearance prompted Paul to experiment further. First he adapted an operation invented by a famous plastic surgeon as a replacement for syphilitic noses. This tremendously complicated procedure involved making a model of a nose, covering it with split skin graft from the thigh, putting it inside the nose to constitute a new lining and later inserting a bone graft. Next he turned his attention to the lack of eyebrows, which persisted even after the disease had burned itself out. Again Paul adapted an operation used first for other reasons, this time one used by an American naval surgeon who had made eyebrows for a Korean war burns victim, by transplanting a piece of scalp. Again the experiment was a triumphant success. Through the years the technique of the team's surgery kept improving. The original tendon transplant used on Krishnamurthy completely changed, to follow a new procedure known as the 'Brand Operation', which gave greater movement and was even less disfiguring. Other problems remained, however, particularly the problem of foot ulcers. Foot ulcers developed both during and after the disease and were caused by the slightest pressure on the feet; the problem of how to eliminate this pressure occupied Brand and his team for years until, after many experiments, they developed moulded shoes which fitted the feet absolutely. Now, providing that the patients and ex-patients checked their feet frequently for any sign of ulceration and always wore the shoes, ulcers could be kept to the minimum.

Another unresearched problem of leprosy was the problem of the involvement of the eye which often resulted in blindness. Stages on the way to blindness included eye-lid paralysis and ineffective tear ducts, both resulting in dry, infected eyes and possible blindness. It was also possible for leprosy itself to invade the eye, usually attacking the first third of the eyeball since it is a surface disease. Cateracts of the eye were also a by-product of leprosy. In 1954 after the birth of her fifth child, Margaret began research into leprous diseases of the eye and eventually developed a series of surgical techniques and treatments which were to prove very effective and lead her to become established in her own right as one of the world's leading authorities on the problems of the eye in leprosy.

Now Paul and Margaret are living in Carvilla, Louisiana, where they are both based at the United State Public Health Hospital, the only institution for the treatment of leprosy in North America. They both continue with their research into the treatment of leprosy as well as travelling the world to publicise developments in this, the field of medicine to which they have both given their lives.

Perhaps the essence of Paul Brand's work is summed up best by a talk he gave one hot evening in Vellore to a group of lepers who lived in a house known as 'Number 10'. Here were housed some of the many patients who swarmed to the leprosy sanatorium to be treated. Many of them destitute beggers, they waited here for their treatment, reviled by the rest of the population of Vellore who found it intolerable that a house for lepers should be allowed in the middle of the bazaar section of town. Sitting in the courtyard surrounded by his patients Paul talked about what he knew best – hands. He reminded them of Christ's crucified hands; 'It hurts me to think of a nail being driven through the centre of any hand,' he said, 'because I know what goes on there, the tremendous complex of nerves and tendons and blood vessels and muscles. It's impossible to drive a spike through its centre without crippling it. Christ was not only able to endure poverty with the poor, weariness with the tired, but – clawed hands with those crippled.' And when Christ was resurrected, Paul reminded the crowd, he kept the stigmata of nails on his hands. 'He carried the marks of suffering so he could continue to understand the needs of those suffering. He wanted to be forever one with us.'